Productivity Equation

The Four Step Process to Accomplishing More of What's Important to You

ELITA TORRES

www.LeadGrowDevelop.com

PRODUCTIVITY EQUATION: The Four Step Process to Accomplishing More of What's Important to You

Copyright © 2018 by Elita Torres.

All rights reserved. Printed in Canada. No part of this book may be used or reproduced in any manner whatsoever without written permission except in the case of brief quotations embodied in critical articles or reviews.

The information contained in this guide is for informational purposes only. If you wish to apply the ideas contained in this book, you are taking full responsibility for your actions.

Although, the author and publisher have made every effort to ensure that the information in this book was correct at press time, the author and publisher do not assume and hereby disclaim any liability to any party for any loss, damage, or disruption caused by errors or omissions, whether such errors or omissions result from negligence, accident, or any other cause.

For information contact:
info@leadgrowdevelop.com

Book and Cover design by Sumamemon
ISBN: 978-1-7753499-0-7 (print)
978-1-7753499-1-4 (electronic)

First Edition: September 2018

DEDICATION

This Book is dedicated to my Husband, Carl. Thank you for always supporting me in all I do. Your belief in me often outweighs what I think is possible.

My sons, Nathan and Wyatt. You are my inspiration for everything I aim to accomplish. The world is better because you are in it. Remember ALWAYS: Never let FEAR stop you from moving forward towards what you want.
Never Give UP! Never Surrender on Your Dreams.

My Mom and Dad.

Dad, thank you for your Legacy of Love and Family. You taught me so much about hard work, courage and love, just by being who you are.

Mom, you introduced me to my world of faith, which without it, so much would not be possible.

To God, all I have done, you have been by my side.

"I can do all things through Christ who strengthens me"

Philippians 4:13

ELITA TORRES

Get the Productivity Lessons Resource as a Thank You for Purchasing my book:

A collection of 5 key articles to start you on your Productivity Journey.

Click the link

https://leadgrowdevelop.lpages.co/productivity-equation-resources

Table of Contents

PRODUCTIVITY EQUATION

CHAPTER ONE – Congratulations! Your Responsibilities Just Increased by 330%	7
PART 1 – RIGHT MINDSET	10
CHAPTER TWO – The Myth of Time Management	11
CHAPTER THREE – Starting with What is Most Important	15
CHAPTER FOUR – Does Life Balance Exist?	21
CHAPTER FIVE – Are You Busy, Or Are You Productive?	32
PART II: RIGHT HABITS	48
CHAPTER SIX – The Fight Between Good Habits and Bad Habits. Who Wins?	39
CHAPTER SEVEN – Personal Habits That Drive Productivity	45
CHAPTER EIGHT – Leadership Habits That Drive Productivity	52
CHAPTER NINE – Planning Habits That Drive Productivity	61
PART III: RIGHT SYSTEMS	65
CHAPTER TEN – Finding Planning Systems That Work For You	66
CHAPTER ELEVEN – 7 Effective Productivity Systems	70

Table of Contents

CHAPTER TWELVE – Productivity APPS to Get You Started	92
CHAPTER THIRTEEN – Email Strategies That Help Bring Your Inbox to Zero	123
PART IV: THE PLAN	129
CHAPTER FOURTEEN – Out of Overwhelm Came The Productivity Equation	130
References	144
About the Author	145
Free Resources	146

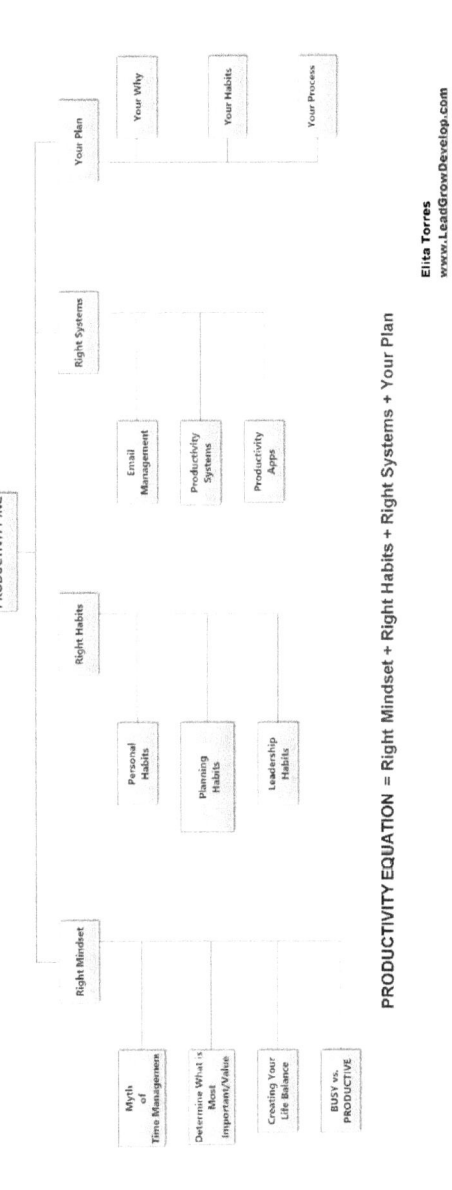

The purpose of this book is to guide you through a process that I call

"The Productivity Equation," which is to help as many people as possible to be productive. To help people determine which tasks they need to focus on today that will bring them the most results tomorrow.

Imagine if you would, a company called, **"Productivity Inc."** As with every company, different components and departments are working together in order to make it successful.

In this company, there are three main divisions.

Mindset Division: To challenge the way we see productivity and "time management."

Habits Division: To help people understand that it is in practicing the right habits that we will see the biggest results.

Systems Division: Once we have the right mindset and habits in place, systems help us maximize productivity.

Every single component is essential in making this company effective. One division relies on the other.

Think of your own productivity in the same way. If you are truly committed to eliminating your Overwhelm, then ensure that you are "recruiting" for every single division of Productivity Inc.

FOREWORD

When it came to finding the right productivity system, the word I would use to describe my persistence is GRIT. According to the Merriam-Webster dictionary, grit in the context of behavior is defined as "firmness of character; indomitable spirit."

I must have tried most of the different productivity systems available; free and paid for, software-based and regular pen and paper-based. I felt like an adventurer looking for the discovered land that had yet to be discovered. Would it be possible?

This book shares what I learned when I went on that adventure. The habits and systems I put in place that finally ended up working for me. I began to notice a pattern. I noticed that while my colleagues were complaining about being overworked, I felt in control. I had learned two steps of the Productivity Equation.

That control continued even when my company restructured, increasing my responsibility by 70%. It was an adjustment, but I applied a few techniques and strategies and quickly bounced back. Within a few weeks of starting this book, I was invited to join several committees.

On top of my regular workload, the following was also added:
- Member of a Product Launch Committee
- Member of Strategic and Planning Committee (a committee charged with ensuring all upcoming initiatives are successful). A committee whose members include Vice Presidents, Buyers, Directors and one District Manager, me.
- Responsible for gathering information and communicating with all the customers and store feedbacks for the Region.

Then the real test came. There was an open position, and I was asked to oversee another district while a replacement was found and trained. My district grew from 13 stores to 23, then 43 stores, all while part of 3

Committees.

This was just at work. I was still balancing maintaining a blog, writing a book and taking care of my two sons, 7 and 11. On top of that, I took on a coaching client whom I met with every Friday night. We met to review and discuss his goals, and I coached him on the actions he should take for the upcoming week.

At one point during that period where I oversaw two districts and 43 stores, I did feel Overwhelmed. All these extra responsibilities came at me at once really putting what I learned to the test. My stress level rose, then kept rising. 80% of the calls I was receiving was from the district I was overseeing, and it was all to communicate problems. I found myself having difficulty keeping all my commitments and it was only week 2 of taking over the second district.

Then, I was having a conversation with someone who told me seven words that flipped a switch on my mindset and made all the difference.

"It's too much for you to handle."

I know that the intention was good. He wanted me to step back and take on less responsibility. What it did instead ignited a spark that burned brighter the more I reflected on those words. It motivated me to look at things differently. I was trying to work the same way as I did before despite the change in environment. I needed to work differently. What worked yesterday, was not going to work today.

> *"Working smart is harder than working hard.*
> *It's just less visible, and we care too much*
> *about what others see." #smartcuts*

Why did those seven words motivate me? I knew I was more than capable of being productive and handling this new workload. I knew that part of my "Overwhelm" came from my mindset and how I looked at the situation.

"The way we see the problem is the problem."

- Stephen R. Covey

I took time to rethink my approach and plan out my new strategy. I laid out my new plan and determined my priorities. This helped me define and act on my next steps.

There are three messages I want to convey in sharing this story:

- Never doubt yourself and never believe someone else's doubt about you.
- When you are faced with an obstacle, sometimes you have to change the lenses that you see through in order to find a way through it.
- Having the right Mindset is the difference maker.

Those seven words only reminded me of what I am capable of. I chose not to believe those words, and it pushed me to want to excel. Did I put too much emphasis on seven simple words? Maybe. Or, was it my competitive nature and desire to be someone who sets a positive example? Either way, it was a motivator, and it set me on a different direction.

It only emphasized the importance of the first step in the Productivity Equation, "Having the right Mindset."

It led me on a path of increased productivity and promotion to Director of Sales. What I learned about productivity was invaluable and allowed me to accomplish more of my goals than ever before.

Two years later, I have only been given more responsibilities, and though there are tough moments, I can still maintain my Productivity levels. I realized that if what I learn can help others, I needed to share my knowledge.

Throughout this book, we will review several tips, tricks, habits, and processes to increase your Productivity. The goal is not to attempt to try everything. You need to experiment with what works for you. You will have the option to choose between several Productivity Habits and

Processes. Work on those that you know will make the biggest difference in reducing your Overwhelm.

I am not a Productivity Guru. I am someone just like you trying to figure things out. Trying to balance and manage all the tasks and responsibilities that come my way. I found an equation that not only worked for me but helped me get further in my career during the last 24 months than in the previous 10 years. As you read through this book, take some notes on what connects with you.

May your Productivity journey propel you further towards your goals.

ELITA TORRES

The Way the Book is Written

Advice given in this book is often presented in list-based formats, which is intended to give a quick snapshot of the information. With the intention of helping you increase your productivity, I felt a list-based format would provide you with a quick reference should you choose to refer back to the book at a later date.

CHAPTER ONE – Congratulations! Your Responsibilities Just Increased by 330%

"Lack of direction, not lack of time, is the problem. We all have twenty-four hour days." – **Zig Ziglar**

Method 1 = Failed
Method 2 = Failed
Method 3....35 = Failed

My Productivity Equation came out of pain. I was overworked and often completed tasks only at the last possible moment. It was overwhelming and frustrating. I knew that if I was going to reach the next level in my personal and professional life, something had to change. I had to change. I needed to find a way to become productive.

I was determined to find the one system that could help me do more in a time where I had less. I tried and failed so many times that I felt like I was the "test dummy" for what didn't work.

My motivation was there at the beginning of every new system I tried. However, when I saw no progress, I would tell myself that the next system will be better. I kept finding myself in the same tailspin over and over.

I was getting more frustrated and losing patience. I couldn't understand it. I was working hard, but at the end of the day, I didn't feel like I was getting anywhere. My to-do list was as long and my Inbox still had over 100 emails, on a good day.

One day when I was helping my youngest son with his homework, I found myself snapping at him extremely quickly because he wouldn't understand the problem quickly enough. He looked at me first with shock, then said, "sorry mommy.". He was sorry? He somehow felt like he disappointed me. That he let me down. I realized that something had to change. My attempt at becoming more productive was putting me out of balance with my life.

I read a lot of books and listened to a few podcasts on the subject. What I came to realize is that I needed to forget about the type of system itself and change my approach to the whole thing.

I needed to:
- Stop focusing on completing my to-do list and think instead about what I was putting on my to-do list.
- Take time to step back and see where I was investing my time and energy.
- Plan my day intentionally.

- Think about my values and determine which habits needed to change immediately.

Once I started focusing on what was truly important and which habits I needed to develop, there was a shift in my mindset. It wasn't about the latest tips, tools or systems that I used. It was that shift in my mindset that made "ALL" the difference.

It was how I treated "time" in itself that counted. I began to realize that how I chose to spend my time was up to me. Increasing my productivity wasn't about getting things done quickly, but about getting the "right" things done when they should be.

I no longer let urgency but importance drive my life. I now let my values drive my planning process, in order to ensure that I am achieving my highest priorities. I chose a planning system, not because it was the most popular but because it fits with my style.

If you are feeling overwhelmed, read the rest of this book and commit to trying new things. Don't be so hard on yourself if you still haven't found the right system. Hopefully, one of these chapters or even a part of this chapter will help guide you to increased productivity.

PART I: RIGHT MINDSET

CHAPTER TWO – The Myth of Time Management

*"Think ahead. Don't let day-to-day operations drive out planning." –
Donald Rumsfeld*

There is one thing that is a big universal equalizer. The ONE thing that we all have exactly the same of, whether rich or poor and no matter in which culture or religion. This big equalizer is time. We all have the same 24 hours in a day. What differentiates a successful person from an unsuccessful one is how they choose to invest those 24 hours.

So where do people get it wrong? They believe that in order to become more productive, they need to become better at Time Management. The problem is, that if you are focusing on time management, you are getting it wrong. You are putting your energy into something that is impossible to do.

The 3 Lies We Tell Ourselves about Time Management:

1. We believe we can get more time by organizing our priorities.
2. We believe we can save Time.
3. We believe time is something that we manage.

No matter how hard you try. No matter how talented you are, you cannot manage time. Time will keep going on at the exact same speed despite your best efforts. It does not speed up or slow down for anyone.

The key to organizing your time more efficiently and increasing your productivity is through self-management.

Take a moment right now and think back to those moments or even days where you felt that no matter how busy you were; you still did not accomplish anything. Those days where you set some ambitious goals for yourself, only to realize that you didn't complete half of what you wanted to do.

What went wrong?

Chances are that if you are thinking about time instead of your priorities, you will have more days like the ones above.

I like Chris Brogan's revision of the word Time Management.

"I work more on time alignment. Is this part of my mission? Does this serve others or strengthen my ability to serve others? Those two questions keep me tight to my map. That's how I best manage my time and priorities."

–*Chris Brogan is a bestselling author and CEO of Owner Media Group*

Be intentional with your time. In order to think about productivity increase, you first need to change your mindset. Start thinking about your values and priorities and work to develop consistent habits that will help you achieve your goals. Productivity is not about getting more things done. Productivity is about accomplishing more towards your KEY goals.

So where do you start?

In order to increase your time alignment, work on your self-management.

PRODUCTIVITY EQUATION

The quickest way to increase your productivity is by replacing your bad habits with good habits.

I was completely at a loss on how to increase my productivity. As I mentioned in chapter 1, I tried almost everything. Then I discovered what I now call, "**The Productivity Equation**."

The rest of this booklet will guide you through the process of this equation.

Productivity Equation = Right Mindset + Right Habits + Right System + Your Plan

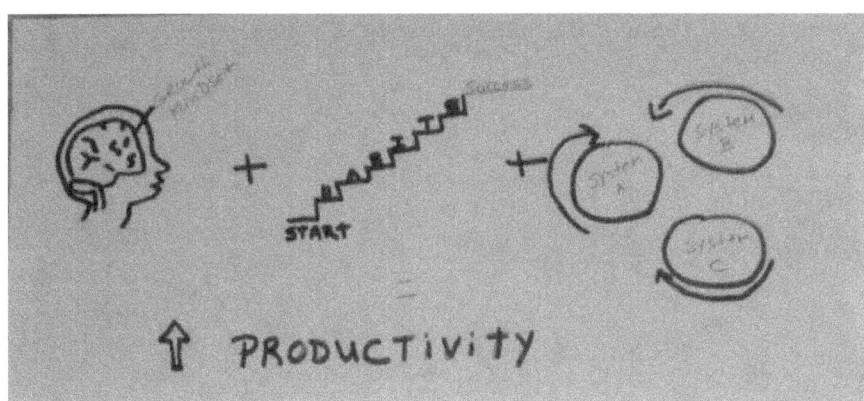

All right. No one said I was an artist. The drawing above is taken from a doodle I created when I was developing my productivity equation. The first step was in changing my Mindset when it came to productivity. Having the right Mindset means:

(i) Determining what your Personal Philosophy is. What matters most?

(ii) Understanding the difference between being Busy vs. being Productive.

(iii) Changing the way you set your goals

Having the right Habits means:

(i) How to effectively plan your day with your MIT.
(ii) Eliminating Distractions
(iii) Weekly Overview

Having the right System for:

(i) Email Management
(ii) Task Management
(iii) Project Management

Starting your plan means:

Putting it all together and beginning.

CHAPTER THREE – Starting with What is Most Important

"If you don't design your own life plan, chances are you'll fall into someone else's plan. And guess what they have planned for you? Not much."
– Jim Rohn

Ever since Robert was 14 years old, he knew that he was going to be a Doctor just like his Dad. He would watch his Dad get dressed in the morning and imagine that it was him. His Dad would tell him how hard he needed to study in order to get his degree.

"Son," he would say. "Your education has to be your number 1 priority if you want to be a Doctor". So he studied hard in school and focused all his energy on getting the best grades that he could. He didn't care about missing all those parties with his friends because he was working on getting his career.

After all those years of studying, all those years sacrificing as an intern, he finally made it. He became a Doctor. His parents were so proud, and his girlfriend finally felt that she would get that proposal. After all, that was the deal they had. She would be patient while he went through school and then she would get her ring.

10 years later, Robert was getting dressed while his 5-year-old son was playing next to him. He looked at himself in the mirror and realized he was not happy. He put all his energy and attention into something that was his Father's dream for him and not his own. He never really stopped to think about what he really wanted. He just "went with the flow." He vowed that day to help his son choose his own destiny. He never took the time to figure out what was important to him.

Robert is a fictional character, but the concept behind the story is real. How many people just "go with the flow" and put their life on auto-pilot? Are you doing today what you really want to do? Are you doing what is most important to you?

Now you may be asking me, "Elita, what does this have to do with productivity?" Well, it depends on how you define productivity.

<u>Business Dictionary</u> (Business Dictionary, n.d.) **defines productivity as:**

"A measure of the efficiency of a person, machine, factory, system, etc., in converting inputs into useful outputs."

If you are reading this book, it probably means that based on the title, you are either feeling overwhelmed or you are looking for ways to become more productive. However, in order to do both, you need to define for yourself what your priorities are. You need to define your, "useful outputs."

The story above may be an exaggerated example of your current situation. However, if you start jotting down how you spend your week, including the minutes and hours you spend doing them, you might be surprised. You might be surprised to find the amount of time you spend on things that are not truly important to you. How much of your time is spent on things that matter most?

Do you even know "what matters most?"

If you were to pause and think seriously about the most important things in your life, what would they be? Are you putting the things that matter least ahead of the things that matter most?

When I understood what my values were, when I got clear on my "most important," it became easier to become more productive. Why? Because I let my values and priorities determine where I would spend most of my energy.

How to Determine What Matters Most

Before you can even begin to increase your Productivity, you need to determine your philosophy and vision first. Don't think about time, think about values, priorities and consistent habits. The aim of being more productive is to let importance, not urgency drive your life.

Our time in this world is limited. You will never get the time you lost yesterday back. How do you want to invest your time today? Hopefully, the answer is held in your most important values.

I first read, "The Seven Habits of Highly Effective People" by Stephen R. Covey (Covey) when I was 16 years old. Until this day, I have yet to come upon an exercise as powerful in determining what is important as the funeral example that starts his chapter on "Principles of Personal Leadership." If you haven't read that book, I highly recommend it. Its principles are timeless and are as valid today as they were when it was first written.

In short, this exercise has you picturing yourself in your own funeral, watching from the side. In the parlor, you are seeing the people that have come to honor you, to express feelings of love and appreciation for your life. You see that there are to be four speakers. The first, from your immediate or extended family – children, brothers, sisters, parents. The second speaker is one of your friends. The third speaker represents a member of your work or profession. And the fourth is from your community. Now, close your eyes and think about what you would like each of these people to say about you.

- What kind of a father or mother do you want to be?
- What kind of a husband or wife?
- What kind of friend?
- Employee? Employer?

What character traits would you like to describe you and what contributions or achievements do you want them to remember?

What a powerful exercise in determining what is important. Another similar exercise is to imagine yourself on your death bed. As you reflect on your life, what do you imagine as your greatest contributions and accomplishments? Will you regret all those plays or games you missed with your kids, or will you wish you spent longer hours in the office?

What is your End Game? What is the end result you want to accomplish? Think forward to 1-5-10 or 30 years from now. What do you want your life to look like? Now picture that life and jot down what comes to mind. What values do you need to focus on to get you there?

Now that you know what is most important, how do you go about achieving it?

It ALWAYS starts with your Mindset.

The Magical Power of Mindset

If you want to renovate or just simply put up a picture, where do you turn to? Probably your toolbox. Your toolbox is usually your go-to place to help you get started on any home renovation project. When we are dealing with our Personal Development, we all have our own "Personal Toolbox." What you store in your personal toolbox is used throughout your life to help you achieve success. Your experience, skills, habits, and mindset are just some examples.

One of the most powerful tools in your arsenal is your mindset. Merriam-Webster defines Mindset (Merriam Webster n.d.) as; "a mental attitude or inclination, a fixed state of mind." Think of every single determining quality required to achieve any high-level result and at the base of it all is your Mindset. (Torres)

Determination

Focus

Passion

Continuing to Pursue your goals despite your Fears

Drive

Patience

Self-Confidence

I can go on and on.

All the above qualities start with having the RIGHT mindset. We are all faced with obstacles and setbacks. You can choose to let it defeat you and keep you from trying to push forward, or you can decide to see it as a learning experience and propel you further.

"There is always a step small enough from where we are to get us to where we want to be. If we take that small step, there's always another we can take, and eventually, a goal thought to be too far to reach becomes

achievable." - Ellen Langer

CHAPTER FOUR – Does Life Balance Exist?

"There is no decision that we can make that doesn't come with some sort of balance or sacrifice."
– Simon Sinek

When it comes to Role Models, my Father has been one of my biggest influencers. Every decision he has ever made stemmed from his desire to provide for his family and give them a better life. Growing up, I remember the countless hours he spent at work to ensure everything was going well. He gave it his all so that his family wouldn't have to want. During the week, we hardly saw him, and when he came home, he was exhausted.

We were not a rich family. In fact, we lived a rather modest life, but all our basic needs were met. Impressive, for an immigrant from Portugal who came over to Canada without knowing anyone. Without knowing the language, he worked his way tirelessly to be able to build a life for himself and one day he hoped, his family. He had a lot of goals for himself, some, he still has not attained. But his greatest asset, according to him, was his wife and six children.

Two years before his full retirement and pension benefits, the company he gave more than 28 years of his life for, restructured and cut his position, leaving him without a retirement plan. He was Banquet Manager at a Hotel and was forced to find a job cleaning tables in a shopping center during the graveyard shift.

This event changed his life and his perception of his worth in the world. I still believe to this day that is one of the significant factors that led to his having a significant stroke less than two years later at the age of 60. He had to retire forcibly and was no longer able to be, "the provider." Forget the fact that 5 of his six children were already out of the home and could take care of themselves. He felt like he could no longer contribute. That he now had less value in the world.

One day, we were having a deep conversation about life when he admitted that he had a lot of anger because he could no longer provide financially. I told him that the way I saw it; it was a blessing. He worked his entire career and spent most of his energy and focus working for what he saw as, being able to give his family a better life. However, he wasn't there "with" his family. Now that his children were adults, they didn't need him financially but needed him emotionally. I encouraged him to see his current situation as a way to spend time on what was truly important. To take advantage of this extra time and get to know who his children were.

My Dad celebrated his 79th birthday this year, and I will never forget his answer to a question I asked. We were toasting to his birthday, and I asked him what accomplishment he was most proud of. His answer, "I am proud of all my children and my wife. They are what makes me proud". It wasn't his accolades and accomplishments in his career; it was his family.

In my Dad's mind, pouring all his energy into his work was for his family. He worked so hard hoping to leave us a Legacy. Today, I wonder if he regrets all those missed moments. I'd like to believe that he no longer feels like he "failed" us when he lost his job. I'd like to believe that he now realizes that all those material possessions he was seeking for his family were not important. That while we were not rich in material possessions, we were rich in love. His Legacy is not financial but has an even greater value.

We hear of the term, "a balanced life" so often that it is important to ask the question, "Does balance really exist?" If so, what does it mean? As much as you try, you cannot do everything at once. There are only 24 hours in a day and the chances that you can spend equal amounts of time in every important area of your life is zero to none.

In fact, just work alone can take up to 8-10 hours of your day, not including travel. If sleep is a part of your daily habits, then deduct another 6-8 hours from your available time. This leaves you 6-10 hours for your remaining roles. It is easy to see that the term, "a balanced life" has nothing to do with the balance of time itself.

"Happiness is not a matter of intensity but of balance, order, rhythm, and harmony." – Thomas Merton

What balance means for me is probably extremely different than what balance means for you. It comes down to our Personal Philosophies (Torres, Four Steps in Determining your personal philosophy) and our values.

There is no perfect formula for balance. For person X, a balanced life might look like this:

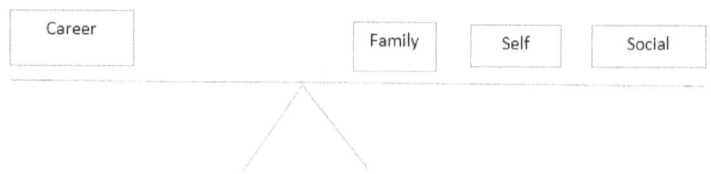

For person Y, a balanced life might look like this:

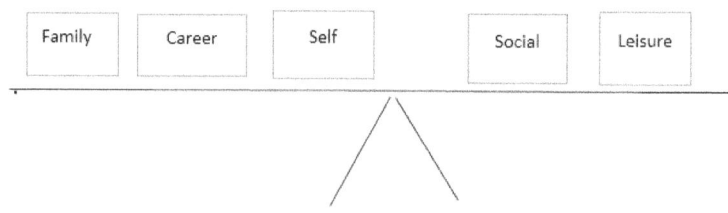

To define what Balance means for you, you need to take into consideration that life is constantly changing. The right balance for you today, may not be the right balance for you the next day. As your life changes, so may your priorities. We have seen many career priorities change with the arrival of a son or daughter. So if balance means different things to different people, how can you achieve balance?

How do you know when you have achieved a balanced life?

The way to determine if your life is in balance is by how you are feeling about the different areas of your life. To have a balanced life means that you have a handle on the various elements in your life. That you don't feel tugged or pulled in any direction. If you were to reflect on any area of your life, you do so with a calm and clear-headed conscious.

The one constant in knowing you have a balanced life is the feeling of accomplishment and happiness. There is no guilt that in spending time in one area, you are sacrificing another area altogether.

Often times, the feeling of being overwhelmed is when we feel out of balance. When one area of our lives is taking too much away from another area of our lives.

Areas You Need to Focus on in Order to Maintain Balance

When you think about productivity, don't think of it in terms of getting the most done in a given time, but getting the right things done. Let your priorities be your compass to set you in the right direction. Then, determine boundaries in each area of your life to maintain your level of balance.

We often are great in creating plans at work and focusing on priorities. After all, it is what we get paid to do. However, we often forget that we don't just have one role to play. Most of our efforts get immersed in the effectiveness of one or two roles, neglecting several other areas of our lives.

When we speak of balance, I am referring to two main areas; Balance of Self and the Balance of External Factors. All other areas or roles we hold fall into one of these two main areas.

Balance of Self

People spend millions of dollars a year in investments; stocks, real-estate and more. As an employee or employer, we invest our time and energy in hopes that there will be a financial return. Why then do so many of us forget to invest in ourselves? Our investment in ourselves is the most important investment we can make.

(i) **Mind:**

How you think and what you know.

Throughout school, you got a formal education. Your ability to keep growing and stretching yourself will come from your continued self-education. Make time for continued knowledge through reading, writing or listening.

While I am on the road traveling, I listen to a variety of podcasts and books on tape that challenge my way of thinking.

(ii) Body:
Your overall physical well-being.

When my car makes the slightest noise or performs less than its best, I make an appointment to have it checked. After all, I rely on it to support my living. Being a Sales Director, I often travel visiting different stores. I cannot afford to let it my car break down.

In contrast, when my fingers started getting numb every once in a while, it took me seven months before I even went to see the Doctor. Even then, once I saw my Doctor, he gave me a paper to run some blood tests. I am even embarrassed to tell you how long that took me.

Why are we better with our possessions than we are with ourselves? Our bodies are our vehicles. Without a healthy body, our capacity and ability to perform gets significantly diminished. We are diligent with our oil changes and maintenance checks but put aside the many benefits of exercise. Your productivity is highly dependent on your health and energy levels.

Don't take your body for granted. What is your plan for exercise, nutrition, and hydration?

(iii) Spiritual:
The search for transcendent meaning. The search for meaning in life events and a yearning for connecting with something larger than oneself.

There is a difference between being spiritual and being religious. You can enhance your spirituality by being more religious, but you don't need to be religious to be more spiritual.

Committing to your values is one way to connect with your spirituality. Do you know your personal philosophy and what are you doing daily to ensure that you have integrity towards your values?

Spirituality can be expressed in many ways; religious practice, music, your relationship to nature, a set of philosophical beliefs or your relationships with friends, family, and community.

External Balance

(i) Family:

Your relationship and connection to your immediate and extended family.

Sometimes the people we love the most are the ones we take most for granted. If the family is high above your list of priorities, make sure you are being intentional about the quantity and quality of time you spend with them. Most often, it is not the amount of time that is important but what you do in that time. Be present in the moment, together.

(ii) Career:

Career does not refer to one position alone but the jobs held and titles earned over a long period of time.

Probably the hardest area to keep in balance with the rest. With companies demanding more and more while providing less resources, sometimes it can be difficult to set and maintain boundaries.

"Investing in productivity in your career will significantly increase your chances of achieving productivity in other areas of your life." - Elita Torres

Once you achieve productivity in your career, maintaining balance is learning to "disconnect" your mind and thoughts when you are no longer at work.

(iii) Social:

Your relationship and connections outside your family. This includes friends, community and your network.

Time is very limited, and it can be important to have a network of people outside your work and family. Just remember that the type of people you interact with influences not only the subject matter you engage in but the level of consciousness that you operate it.

"You are the average of the five people you spend the most time with." – Jim Rohn

How many parents warn their children about the friends they choose to hang out with? How many of those same parents take their own advice?

(iv) Leisure:

Time spent not working

Yes, taking time off is significantly important. People fall into the trap of thinking they can't afford to take time off. Look at it in the way that you can't afford NOT to take time off.

Taking time to rejuvenate and refill your energy is important to maintaining balance. How you choose to energize is up to you; bike riding, dancing, nature walks or hikes.

Here's another important piece of advice, "It's o.k to take a vacation." (Torres, 7 Great Tips About Taking Vacations n.d.)

Here are some stats:

- There was a Google Consumer Survey conducted in the first few days of 2015. They asked 1,500 American adults how many vacation days they took last year. Nearly 42 percent of people reported not using a single day of their ten average allotted vacation days.
- Careers website Glassdoor (Glassdoor n.d.) and Harris Interactive took a poll of 2,300 workers who get paid vacation. Only 25% said they use all their paid days each year and 61% said that while they're on vacation, they continue to work. A quarter of respondents said that a colleague got in touch with work while they were on vacation and 20% heard from their boss.
- Another survey by Expedia, (Expedia n.d.) measured vacation deprivation by country. Which countries were the most vacation

deprived? United States, Canada, Mexico, Singapore, Japan and South Korea. Americans earn fewer vacation days than people in most countries but still leave two days unused on average. Canadians earn fewer vacation days as well but tend not to accumulate any vacation days.

Taking a break is essential for your creativity and has actually been proven to increase your productivity.

When it comes to balancing, remember the Law of the Harvest: We always reap what we sow. If you neglect certain areas of your life, weeds will grow.

Balance is also about the ability to live in the moment. The way to ensure one area does not encroach in another area is to "Be Present" wherever you are.

The following is an excerpt of a Blog Post I wrote about, "The Importance of Living in The Moment." (Torres, Living in The Moment n.d.)

The Importance of Living in The Moment

Are you the type of person who lives in the moment, or do you try to live in several moments at once? Of course, this cannot be done effectively. I mentioned during a recent post that I went on a cruise. Sure there were tons of activities to do, but the moments I enjoyed most were those where I was 100% present.

Often, our physical body is in one place, but our mind is in another place altogether. You may be at work thinking about what you want to do during the weekend, or at home, thinking about what you want to accomplish at work.

Have you ever been out to dinner with your family, but spent your time answering emails, texting, or worse, on social networks? I have been guilty of that too at some point.

If you catch yourself in that situation, STOP. Take the time instead to be truly present in the moment. If it is important enough to be present physically, then it is important enough to be there mentally.

If you are around other people, what message are you sending when you are mentally somewhere else? What kind of withdrawal are you making in the relationship bank account?

Be present in the moment, no matter how many other responsibilities are calling your attention elsewhere. Put your priorities where you are physically, and you may be surprised what can come out of it.

A more enriched relationship

Deeper personal connections
Getting to truly understand the person fully
Immense deposits into the relationship

If you are at work, but your mind is elsewhere, how productive can you truly be? It is said that multitasking is not as effective as focusing your attention on one thing at a time.

"We are the generation capable of doing many things at once, without enjoying any of them."

– Dinesh Kumar Biran

The same is true if you are at work, but not focused. Give your attention and energy to the task at hand and reap the rewards.

The point is, wherever you are, BE THERE. Take part in the conversation. It was moments such as those when I took in the scene of the ocean lapping the ship or watching my kids having a great time on the water slides that I will cherish. The conversations my family and I had over a meal were my favorites. No distractions, no electronics.

When I asked my kids what their favorite part was, they told me, "all the family time."

PRODUCTIVITY EQUATION

"If you are living a life out of balance, then you are not living a life of full potential." - *Elita Torres*

If you are out of balance, the first thing to do is Stop and figure out what needs to be done to regain control. Take time to realign with your values and what is truly important. This an important step. If you are able to reconnect with your Personal Philosophy and your MOST important areas, then you can gain the MOTIVATION you need to make a change.

ELITA TORRES

CHAPTER FIVE – Are You Busy, Or Are You Productive?

"It is not enough to be busy... The question is: what are we busy about?" - **Henry David Thoreau**

It was the winter of 1993 and 19-year-old me was super excited to have her first car. Already imagining all the freedom, it would give me, I was ready for my first winter without having to rely on public transportation. What I wasn't prepared for were the lessons it would teach me.

The car was a 1980 Cutlass Supreme. Yes, it was an old car, and the seat was stuck in the furthest back position, forcing me to sit without resting by back. I didn't care; it was mine. I would take it to college and give rides to my friends. It was Awesome.

Then, during one cold Canadian winter storm, I went to the store with my sister and friend. I parked in the parking lot, and we went inside to go shopping. The weather was bad, but at least we didn't have to wait for the bus. The car was already filled with snow by the time we got back. I got in, started the car and tried to pull out of the parking lot. The car didn't move. I was Stuck, with a Capital S.

It was my first experience being stuck in the snow, and I tried everything. I pressed hard on the accelerator hoping that I could gain enough speed that I would shoot out of the snow bank. Eventually, a stranger offered to try and help get my car out. He climbed in and rocked the car back and forth, back and forth. The car wouldn't budge. It made me feel better that this man in his 40's who I assumed had several years of experience wasn't having any more success than I was.

He was spinning the wheels and pushing the car so hard that I saw smoke coming from the front of the car. I asked him to stop and thanked him for trying. I think I bruised his ego because he reluctantly left the driver's seat.

Finally, giving up on finding a technique, we walked to the nearest gas station and bought some salt and tire treads. Eventually, we were able to release the car from the snow's tight grip. I learned soon after that I was doing a lot of things wrong.

What is one of the most important things to do when your car is stuck in a snow bank? At 19, I didn't know the answer. Today I do.

"The most important thing to do is not to spin the wheels."

Step 1, in getting "unstuck" is to try as much as possible to remove snow from your undercarriage and tires. Then, the key is to put your car in the lowest possible gear and *gently* press on the accelerator. If you are still stuck, the idea is to gently rock the car back and forth with the intent to gain momentum.

I thought the key lay in pushing the accelerator as hard as the car could handle when really, it was about technique.

You work hard, extremely hard. You push on that accelerator as hard as you can handle. At the end of your day, do you look at the list of things you've done and feel like you didn't accomplish anything? Do you find yourself in this scenario often? If you do, then although you may be extremely busy, you may not be productive. You may be accomplishing a lot of tasks, but it may not be sending you towards the right direction. In fact, just like the tires on my car, you might be digging yourself in deeper.

Take a few moments now and think about your last day at work. What are you most proud of accomplishing?
Why?

Chances are what you were most proud of accomplishing contributed greatly to your most important goals.

People need to feel a sense of accomplishment, so they work long hours and put as much into their workday as possible. They believe that busyness will get them success.

What if you could switch your focus from being busy to being productive? What if your aim was not to accomplish the greatest number of tasks but the right tasks?

"Success is not about the volume of tasks you accomplish but the relevancy of tasks." – Rory Vaden

Make the shift in mindset when you are planning your day. Be intentional about what the day needs to look like.

> BEFORE THE DAY EVEN STARTS, WHAT ARE THE 2-3 TASKS THAT MUST ABSOLUTELY GET DONE?

Notice, how I didn't say 10-20 tasks?

Remember Pareto's Principle: Roughly 80% of effects come from 20% of causes.

Figure out what that 20% represents to your day then repeat the same process every day.

> *"Someone who plans their day intentionally can get more things done in 5 hours, then someone who works 9 hours without a plan."* Elita Torres

Before I became a District Manager, I was the General Store Manager of a Hudson's Bay Store. They are a major department store who is also part of a large family of other retailers such as Lord & Taylor and Saks Fifth Avenue.

When executives would come and visit, I may have put in 1-2 extra hours in the week, but I ran the store as if nothing was changing. I remember a colleague of mine who was the manager of another store, who used to work 50-60 hours during the week of the visit. I never understood why? The end result was similar; we both were always given great reviews.

It wasn't because I wasn't passionate about my job or fully engaged that I worked fewer hours than my colleague. I tried to build a culture in my store that was visit ready, every day. When I would first take over a store, I would work extra hours with the intent that the hours I put in today would result in fewer hours tomorrow.

My first step would be in creating my winning team. If I could help "Build a High-Performance Team," my time would be multiplied. I invested my time into things every day that would create more time in the future.

Within a short time, I no longer needed to work an enormous number of hours to get my store ready for an executive visit. I invested my time into what would bring me the greatest return. I was focused on being Productive instead of Busy.

> *"Multiply your time by giving yourself permission to invest time into things today that will create more time tomorrow."* - Rory Vaden

Want to be more productive? Then first start by understanding the difference between being busy and being productive.

The 6 Major Differences Between Busy People and Productive People:

1. Priorities

Busy People have many priorities. Productive People have very few priorities. Their mission is clearly defined, and they put their energy on the few items that will bring them the biggest results.

2. Yes, Vs. No

Busy People say yes quickly. Productive People say Yes slowly. They don't commit to anything that steers them away from their mission and goals.

3. Handling of Actions

Busy People focus on actions and checking things off of their To-Do list. Productive People focus on clarity before action and have very few things on their To-Do list.

4. Multi-Task Vs. Focus

Busy People are always multi-tasking. Productive People don't multitask but focus on one course until completion.

5. Email Management

Busy People respond quickly to emails. Productive People don't allow emails to determine their priorities. They don't allow other people to manage their day and are not distracted by the incoming email alerts.

6. Question they Ask Themselves

Busy People ask, "What else can I add?" Productive People ask, "What else can I remove?" At the beginning of the day, they determine what needs to be their most important tasks of the day, in line with their goals. Then, throughout the day, they take the time to review their priorities and eliminate or delegate anything that doesn't align with their vision.

PRODUCTIVITY EQUATION

PART II: RIGHT HABITS

CHAPTER SIX – The Fight Between Good Habits and Bad Habits. Who Wins?

"Chains of Habit are too light to be felt until they are too heavy to be broken." – Warren Buffett

My Husband and I took my children to Disneyworld and Universal Florida in the Summer of 2013. They were 8 and 4 years old. Recently, we were discussing the new addition to Universal Studios, "The Wizarding World of Harry Potter," and how we had missed the opportunity to see it since it had yet to be built.

My sons were reminiscing about all the cool rides they were able to go on and those that they were too small to ride. They could vividly remember the rides that they wanted to go on but didn't meet the height requirements.

My oldest son Nathan talked about that one ride that he wanted to go on so badly but was two inches too small. Curious, he asked if he would still be too small to ride it today. He remembered that it required you to be 51 inches tall and that his height at that time was 49 inches.

I grabbed a measuring tape and measured both of my boys. Since we don't keep track of heights on a wall, Nathan was amazed at how much he had grown. He now measured 56 inches, a whole 7 inches taller. We then realized that Wyatt was now the height Nathan was at the time of our trip and he too had grown about 6 inches.

I went to our family vacation wall and showed them a picture of us standing together. Wyatt noticed how on the picture he reached my elbow, but now almost grasped my shoulder. The look on his face was almost like his growth was magic.

I must admit, I was pretty surprised as well. Based on the clothes I kept having to buy because they outgrew them, I knew they had apparently grown. But when comparing their height to a particular point in time such as our trip, it was pretty amazing.

"You don't realize all the growth or change that is happening in the moment, but when you compare your personal growth to a point in history, it can amaze."

– Elita Torres

My son Nathan is one of the shortest of his friends. It sometimes makes him feel "small." I try to encourage him that he still has many years in which he will continue to grow. I know it can sometimes discourage him. When he saw how much he had grown, it put a smile on his face. He realized that while he cannot see his growth happening, he now knew that his body was working on it every day.

We all have Habits, some were intentionally and some unintentionally formed. We are not always conscious of the process in which habits are formed. Our routines form our habits, and by repeating the same routines, eventually, they will become engrained in our minds.

We sometimes let ourselves perform actions that we know are not in our best interests, thinking, "Ah, it is only one time. One cheesecake or one cigarette won't hurt." What we are not realizing is that we are slowly building a routine. Then, much like my sons who grew all those inches by what seemed like magic, our routines turn into habits.

The good thing about habits is that we can choose which ones we keep and which ones we change. Once you understand that fact, you have the freedom and the responsibility to remold them. By understanding that habits can be rebuilt, the power of habit becomes easier to grasp.

As a high school student, I was proud of the fact that one of my values was not to speak ill of anyone behind their back. A few years later, I was having a drink with a college friend who often gossiped about a few of our other friends. In fact, it was something that nearly all of my friends did. I would normally sit back and listen, but this one particular day, I joined in. She laughed. It felt good to make her laugh, so a few times after that; I repeated this behavior a couple of more times. Eventually, I became the person who would call someone up to rant about something someone else did.

I am not sure when it finally kicked in. The realization that I too became someone who gossiped. A part of me mourned that high school student who was so proud of her values. When did I lose that value? It snuck up on me, but it now became one of my bad habits.

> *"Habits are formed by the repetition of particular acts. They are strengthened by an increase in the number of repeated acts. Habits are also weakened or broken, and contrary habits are formed by the repetition of contrary acts."* - Mortimer J. Adler

It can be easier to form a bad habit than it is to form a good habit and you have to work twice as hard to destroy your bad habits. After all, the rewards of eating that cheesecake are so good.

The reason why we indulge in bad habits is because most of the time, our consequences are not immediate. They are slow in growing and in revealing themselves.

If you want to increase your productivity and multiply your time, the quickest way is to replace those bad habits preventing you from achieving your goals. You need to replace those unproductive habits with productive ones.

"Your net worth to the world is usually determined by what remains after your bad habits are subtracted from your good ones." – Benjamin Franklin

How do you eliminate your bad habits? You have two choices.

Your first choice is to FOCUS all your attention on removing them. If you smoke, you can work hard to stop smoking. Your second choice is to FOCUS all your attention on replacing your BAD habit with a GOOD one.

By focusing on creating GOOD habits, you will eventually replace the BAD habits with GOOD ones.

"We are what we repeatedly do. Excellence, then, is not an act, but a habit." - Aristotle

When I wanted to stop my habit of gossiping, I focused on saying one good thing about the person that was being spoken badly of. Or, I focused on being the person that changed the subject immediately. Eventually, it became who I was again. I also noticed that people stopped gossiping around me because I no longer joined in.

In High School, I was proud that I didn't participate in gossiping. What I didn't realize then is that my silence was enabling the behavior. So instead, I focused on setting the example.

If you want to know more about how to create or change a habit, Charles Duhigg wrote an excellent book titled, "The Power of Habit." (Duhigg n.d.) The book uses scientific discoveries to explain why habits exist and how they can be changed.

The basic premise is that our brain will try to make almost any routine into a habit because habits allow our minds to ramp down. The MIT researchers that he refers to in the book discovered a simple neurological loop at the core of every habit. If you can understand this framework than this three-step loop can be modified to either change or create a new habit.

Cue: A trigger that tells your brain to go into automatic mode and which habit to use.

Rewards: Helps your brain determine if this loop is worth repeating.

Routine: Can be physical, mental or emotional.

The Habit Loop:

Over time, this loop – cue, reward, routine become more and more automatic. Once a habit forms, the brain stops fully participating in decision-making.

The book goes much more into detail, and I highly recommend you read it.

There is a famous Cherokee Legend of Two Wolves that have been told and modified to express many different messages. When you are reading this story, think of it regarding Bad Habits vs. Good Habits.

"A Legend of Two Wolves"

An old Cherokee is teaching his grandson about life.

"A fight is going on inside me," he said to the boy.

"It is a terrible fight, and it is between two wolves. One is evil – he is anger, envy, sorrow, regret, greed, arrogance, self-pity, guilt, resentment, inferiority, lies, false pride, superiority, and

ego." He continued, "The other is good – he is joy, peace, love, hope, serenity, humility, kindness, benevolence, empathy, generosity, truth, compassion, and faith. The same fight is going on inside you – and inside every other person, too".

The grandson thought about it for a minute and then asked his Grandfather, "Which one will win?"

The old Cherokee simply replied, "The one you feed."

Which Habit will you Feed?

The following next three chapters will focus on the Productivity Habits that you need to create in order to multiply your time.

I have divided them into three categories: Personal Habits, Planning Habits, and Leadership Habits.

CHAPTER SEVEN – Personal Habits That Drive Productivity

"I insist on a lot of time being spent, almost every day, to just sit and think. That is very uncommon in American business. I read and think. So I do more reading and thinking and make fewer impulse decisions than most people in business. I do it because I like this kind of life." - Warren Buffett

During our Cruise to Bermuda, we ate at one of the restaurants on the ship. I don't even remember its name, but I do remember the Chocolate Molten Lava Cake. Even as I write this, I can almost remember its taste. It was THAT good.

Do you have a meal or dessert that you can still practically taste? Now imagine trying to recreate that perfect dish. What steps would you take?

- You would first try and find the recipe or one that comes close.
-

- Then you would buy the ingredients.
- After the first two steps, you would try and create your own mouth watering dish.

What would happen if while you were recreating your dish, you realized that you had forgotten one main ingredient? No matter how strong your intentions and desires were to make the perfect cake, without the right tools or resources, you wouldn't have much success.

When it comes to increasing your Productivity, or any other goal you desire to achieve, your HABITS are your tools and resources.

"Without the right Habits, you will find yourself returning to the starting line over and over again."

In the next few pages and chapters, I will be reviewing several Habits that if you work on will improve your productivity.

Here is the IMPORTANT thing to remember. Do not attempt to improve on these Habits all at once. It will discourage you more than anything else. The Key is to start with 1-2 Habits that you can work on today that will make the biggest impact. These are just some of the good habits that can replace your bad habits.

There are probably several habits that you are already doing. If so, that is great. Now, FOCUS on those that you NEED to do next. It does not have to be huge changes.

"The Difference Maker is not usually MAJOR changes, but small daily habits that add up."

Don't aim for perfection, just forward progress. Each decision you make today and every day will either be a small daily deposit or withdrawal towards your success. If you work on a few productivity habits at a time, it will add up. Think of it in terms of having the same effect as "The Power of Compound Interest."

Imagine at the age of 16 years old; you made a decision to *start a savings account. You started putting away $100 a month into an investment account that has a return of 5%. You aim to keep putting in the same amount every month until you are 50.*

Your total investment is ($100 x 12 months) x 34 years = $40,800, but that is not what you end up with.

With the Power of Compound Interest, your actual total money at the end is $107,902 or a total Interest gained of $67,102.

Your Output outweighs your Input by 64%. You put in a total of $40,800 and received an additional $67,102. I wish I would have started that investment idea at 16.

The daily decisions and actions you make every day towards achieving new Habits will add up and give you a greater return than you put in.

13 Personal Habits for Productivity

FOCUS

John Lee Dumas often talks about his definition of FOCUS on his Podcast, "Entrepreneur On Fire." He defines FOCUS as, "Follow One Course Until Success." How many projects have you started and left uncompleted because you decided to take on a different one? By focusing on one priority at a time, you are not splitting your focus and energy. You will get more done both short term and long term.

Minimize Distractions

This is still a huge opportunity for me that I constantly need to work on. Do you get easily distracted? When you are working on a task, minimize any distractions that will impact your productivity. Shut off your notifications and even your phone.

Reorganize your Work Space

If it takes you some time just to figure out where things are, you need to start thinking about how you can reorganize your workspace. One of the first things that I recommend to any of my managers in a new store is that they reorganize their back room. It reduces clutter and improves productivity significantly.

Health Habits

The right health habits play a vital and crucial role in keeping a high level of productivity. If you get a bad night's sleep and wake up tired, you are already setting yourself up for a less productive day. Sleep is the #1 secret to avoiding burnout.

Exercise and a healthy diet is also an important ingredient to your productivity. Did you ever have a heavy lunch, only to attend a meeting after? How focused were you right after the meal? Instead, replace those heavy foods with energy producing foods.

Some examples of foods that boost energy are almonds, dark chocolate, bananas, salmon, coconut and whole grains.

Maximize Commute Time

Whether or not you commute by public transportation or car, you can maximize your commute time in several ways.

Taking the train? Use this time to catch up on emails or plan your priorities for the day. Do you drive to work? Reflect on what key topics you want to emphasize during that all important conversation you've scheduled with your direct report.

Or use your commute time to recharge by listening to some great music, an audiobook or podcast.

Eliminate Time Vampires

Time Vampires refers to anything or anyone that "sucks" your time much like a vampire would suck blood. They can be a major detractor from your productivity and can come in the form of tasks or people. Are there people in your circle that continuously steal from your time without permission? Do you have a colleague that interrupts your work without thought to your day? How about all those unplanned last minute meetings that take you away from what you were working on?

Other examples of Time Vampires are: Social Media sites, checking your emails throughout the day, some phone calls or anything else that distracts you from your priorities.

Master Your Skills

When the company that I worked for introduced a new Software for measuring results, it was a big drain on some people in the beginning. They were frustrated with the new process, and it took a while to get used to it. Those who took the time right in the beginning to be curious and learn new techniques, found themselves catapulting ahead of others when it came to maximizing this new tool.

If there is any software, process or tool that you need to use in your daily business, then take the time necessary to master your skills in that area. It will result in a lot less frustration and increased results. Be curious.

Say No

You are always saying no to something. Either you are saying no to someone's priorities, or you are saying no to your own priorities. You can never be fully productive if you take on too many tasks. You will be spreading yourself too thin. Develop criteria that need to be met in order for you to tackle a new project or task.

Be intentional to what you are saying Yes to as well. Are you saying yes to something that is driving you away from achieving your goals or impacting your energy levels?

Delete Limiting Thoughts

My biggest critic has always been myself. You might be asking yourself, "what does that have to do with productivity and being overwhelmed?" Productivity is about having a bigger output than you put in. We have already covered dozens of examples of what can limit your productivity. However, sometimes the biggest deterrent is your mindset. What you believe is possible or impossible will go a long way to what you can make possible.

Some examples of limiting beliefs are; "I can't, I mustn't, I don't." When you hear these limiting beliefs in your mind, replace them with empowering beliefs. Replace, "I can't do it" with "I can't do it yet." It can be amazing how the right mindset and beliefs can catapult your productivity just by allowing you to know it is possible.

Arrive Early

Starting before anyone else is one way to boost your productivity immensely. If you arrive early and start on your "Most Important Tasks" first, you will allow time for unforeseen obstacles.

Journaling

Journaling is a popular practice amongst the most successful entrepreneurs. Jim Rohn, one of the most popular motivational speakers of all time believed so strongly in the power of journaling that he spoke to it all the time.

> *"If you're serious about becoming a wealthy, powerful, sophisticated, healthy, influential, cultured and unique individual, keep a journal. Don't trust your memory. When you listen to something valuable, write it down. When you come across something important, write it down."* – Jim Rohn

The idea is to keep track of what works, what inspires you or what doesn't work in order to ensure you continue on the right path to your goals. Try journaling for a week and see if you receive any benefits from it.

Take a Time Out

Sometimes, the fastest way to get to your destination is to stop at the pit stop along the road. If you are driving on all cylinders, eventually you will be running on steam. Schedule time to recharge your internal battery so you can focus more clearly after. When your mind is tired, you are not as productive. Think about all the great ideas that come to you in the shower when you are relaxed and not trying so hard. A long walk can help clear the cobwebs of frustration that can come when exhaustion sets in.

Celebrate

We can sometimes be so busy trying to meet all the demands put on us that we can get discouraged when we look ahead. We might still be far from the finish line. Take a moment, and reflect on all you have accomplished. Celebrate all your micro goals and steps along the way. It is all about continued progress and as you keep moving the needle, take the time to recognize all the steps you have already made. This will help you stay productive and on track through the more difficult moments.

CHAPTER EIGHT – Leadership Habits That Drive Productivity

"The mediocre teacher tells. The good teacher explains. The superior teacher demonstrates. The great teacher inspires." William Arthur Ward

I was discussing with a Retail District manager who oversaw 15 locations. We were touring together to identify opportunities in the district. Jennifer expressed her discontent at the visual execution in her stores. She felt that her Store Managers were having difficulty maintaining high visual standards and needed to be better merchants. When we arrived at one of her stores, she started moving fixtures around to emphasize better what was selling. Jennifer spent about an hour and a half making visual changes. In the end, she showed her manager the changes she made.

PRODUCTIVITY EQUATION

When we broke for lunch, I challenged her as to why she made all the changes herself. She replied that when she walked in, she noticed several areas that needed attention. Jennifer said, "Visual execution is so important to the sales in the store. When the brand message is clear, and the shopping experience for the customer is smooth, sales go up."

I agreed with her, but my challenge remained. I again asked why she didn't involve her manager in any of the decisions. Or even better, why she didn't show her manager strategies in becoming a better merchant. Jennifer exclaimed, "Oh no, I tried that before, but it takes too long. It takes longer to explain than to do it myself". Still convinced she didn't understand my message I asked her how often she has to perform this exercise in her stores. "Every time," she answered. I then probed further with, "Do you ever have to do the same exercise in the same store?"

I think you can probably imagine her answer. Of course, she has to repeat the same exercise because she never took the time to teach. She may have thought she was saving time. What she was actually doing was trading shorter time today for longer time tomorrow.

> *"When leaders choose to do tasks themselves without delegating or developing others first, they are trading immediate time gain for greater returns long-term."*

If you are serious about avoiding Overwhelm and increasing your productivity, you need to develop certain leadership habits. Even if you don't have an official leadership title, the term leader applies to anyone who can influence.

> *"Leadership is a process of social influence which maximizes the efforts of others, towards the achievement of a goal." –*
> *Kevin Kruse*

For the purpose of this chapter, I am referring to leadership as a process of maximizing the efforts of others as well as yourself. After all, how can you be an effective leader if you cannot begin to influence your efforts?

5 Leadership Habits That Drive Productivity

1. Delegate

In his book Entreleadership by Dave Ramsey, he uses a rope as a visual to convey the concept of delegation. In his analogy, the rope represents responsibility. When it comes to delegation, Dave suggests we hand someone the rope and feed it to them until all we have left is the end of the rope.

What we intend to often do instead is throw the entire rope at the person and hope she knows what to do with it. Delegation, when done properly can be an extremely effective way to increase your productivity. When I was given ten more stores to manage, an increase of 70%, I had to work differently. I learned that I needed to delegate tasks and projects to people who can perform the job as good if not better than myself.

"Effective Delegation is your reward for investing in People Development."

Step 1 is to be able to "Let Go." Let go of the need to control and do everything yourself. Learn to trust in your team, in your ability to effectively delegate and your team's ability to achieve results. Switch the equation around.

Remember that with productivity, your goal is to invest today in actions that will significantly multiply your time tomorrow. You are investing in the future and not so worried about your returns today.

Learning when and what to delegate is the key to effective delegation. Delegate the tasks that are least important so that you can spend more time on what is most important. It does not imply that you delegate non-important tasks. These tasks you should try to eliminate if they do not lead you to your goals.

Delegate to those who have the potential to do the job effectively even if there is a learning curve. The more you delegate to the right people, the quicker they will learn and the greater the returns.

2. Outsource

Sometimes the right person is not someone on your team or household. There will be times when outsourcing is your best solution. Here are three valid reasons for choosing to outsource.

When what you do with your time saved brings in a greater return than your investment in outsourcing. The return on your investment is relative to each individual and does not necessarily have to be a financial return. Imagine you decide to hire a housekeeper twice a month so you can enjoy more quality time with your family. Those few extra hours of quality time can mean deeper and more meaningful relationships which have no monetary value but can be priceless in terms of emotional value.

When your skill level or that of your team members on particular task results in a lack of efficiency or profitability. There are experts available for almost every single task you may want to accomplish. When you don't have enough experience or knowledge, you can decide to learn the skill or outsource it. In writing this book, I didn't even begin to imagine how I would create my own book design. I knew it would be something that I would need to outsource. Design is not my strong suit. In fact, it frustrates me when I try to design something myself. The time it would take to learn how to create anything decent could be spent in creating more content for the book or future projects.

CRM is a huge priority for most customers. It has to be if companies want to survive in today's markets. Salesforce understood this and became the expert in creating a software that connects companies to their customers, partners and employees like never before. Companies can choose to develop their own CRM division. They can invest in creating their own software, learn through trial and error and maybe eventually get it right. Or, they can hire the experts that are getting it right already.

When you have no passion for the task, or when spending time on it will create unnecessary stress. As I previously mentioned, Design is not something that I am passionate about, so when I can, I outsource it. If there is something that needs to get done but will drive you crazy doing it, outsource it to someone else.

3. Network

What does networking have to do with Productivity? Having a wide network that you can refer to can save you tons of time. It can be like the rabbit you pull out of your hat in times of need.

What types of networks should you start to build today?

Recruitment Network: If you are in a leadership position and having to hire talent on an occasional basis, remember the rule, "Always Be Recruiting." You should always be on the lookout for Top Talent and keep a good bank of potential Future Players. This way, if a position opens up, you don't need to spend weeks or months looking for the right person. It can save you a lot of lost time in the future.

Mastermind Network: A Mastermind is a group of individuals who are seeking a common goal. There are several Mastermind groups available to join. A word of caution, make sure you pick a Group that is right for you. Especially, if there is a financial investment involved, ensure your ROI will be present. Look for a Group whose leader has a proven track record of success in the area you strive to improve on. The leader should not only possess the competencies but should also have the capacity to Coach. The Mastermind should also have a set training schedule with key subjects to be covered on a monthly basis.

The greatest advantage of joining a Mastermind group to your productivity is in having an Accountability partner. Someone who you can connect with on a weekly basis and review where you stand on your goals. It is the secret of why Weight Watchers works so well. Having an accountability partner that challenges you to set the right goals and perform the right actions will drive you to be more productive. A group of individuals that understand where you are coming from can propel you further than if you were "going it alone."

Mentorship/Coaching Network: Similar to a Mastermind group but more of a one on one communication. Do you have a mentor?

4. Follow-Up on the Process

If you decide to delegate or outsource some of your tasks, ensure you schedule touch bases for follow-up. Mistakes we often make is passing off tasks to others and then not following up. Schedule one on one times where you can follow up on all projects delegated or outsourced. This can be a great opportunity to recognize great work or coach team members along the way.

"What gets measured, gets done" Ken Blanchard

5. Before Scheduling that Meeting, Does It Pass the Test?

One of the complaints that I hear most often is how there can be too many meetings. No matter in which industry, meetings tend to be a frustration and can be seen as a deterrent to productivity.

Have you ever heard the following terms to describe a meeting: "pointless, waste of time, repetitive, or boring"? The truth is that some meetings are essential. If done properly, they can help unite a team towards a common goal and increase productivity. So why are they often seen as time wasters? In order for a meeting to be productive, it must pass the test.

A productive meeting meets the following criteria:
- Recognizes progress

- Establishes next course of action

Here are 6 Steps You Can Take to Ensure Both Criteria are met:

Set Objectives: Set clear objectives for what having the meeting should accomplish. If the objectives aren't clear, then you can't measure its effectiveness. Keep it simple and summarize the objective in 1-2 sentences. The objective should answer the question, "We are here to…. ".

Provide an Agenda: Show people you respect their time by letting them know which points are to be discussed. The agenda should not only cover the topics that are to be discussed but help determine the flow. If the meeting is a standard fixed meeting, there is no need for an agenda as the structure is already in place.

Assign Action Items / Review Minutes: At the start, review the notes from the previous meeting including commitments discussed. This is a great way to review progress and increase accountability from each member. If members are used to having to report their progress, they will be motivated to want to communicate great results.

Throughout the meeting, action items should be assigned along with clear expectations. Ensure there is someone who is taking notes and that the end of the meeting is used to recap these items. Have the person who is reading them off begin with verbs such as, "Review, Complete, Call, etc...." Set an expected end date for each item as well as the person responsible for completing each item.

Come Prepared: If the initiator of the meeting arrives unprepared, what does that say about its importance? I have been to meetings where the leader is shuffling through his papers looking for a point he wanted to get across. This not only shows disrespect for each attendees' time but can quickly ruin the flow of a meeting. Take the time that is necessary to prepare for the meeting, including how you plan to meet the meeting's objectives.

Examine Your Meeting Process: Reflection and Feedback are key to any progress. Consistently running effective and efficient meetings takes practice. Start the process by ensuring that each meeting can answer the following questions:

"What worked well?"

"What can we improve for the next meeting?"

"Were the meeting objectives met?"

Set and Observe Meeting Rules: There are three rules that you should respect as much as possible when it comes to meetings. If you can respect these three rules, you will eliminate some of the biggest annoyances when it comes to meetings.

(i) **Distractions** - It is easy to lose the attention and focus of the attendees when there are side conversations happening and the sound of fingers tapping away at their phones. Make it a rule to have no electronics unless it is used solely for the purpose of taking notes.

(ii) **Set Start & Stop Times** - Meetings should start on time and stop on time. Simple enough as a rule? Sure, but a rule that is often broken. If the meeting starts at 9 a.m., then start it at 9 a.m. Set the example of respecting commitments by committing to the time agreed on to start the meeting.

Don't run the meeting longer than was scheduled. Not overreaching when planning your agenda will help. If the meeting is scheduled to last an hour but goes on for 90 minutes, chances are the attention span of the last 30 minutes will drop. It goes back to respecting people's time. You will gain lots of points if you get this right.

(iii) **Determine Next Meeting Date** – It can get complicated to find a time that works for everyone. Take advantage while everyone is in the room to gain agreement on the next meeting date.

Leaders play a crucial role in helping their teams stay productive.

Not only are they responsible for the effectiveness of their team, but in order to remain effective, they need to learn first to Lead themselves.

CHAPTER NINE – Planning Habits That Drive Productivity

" Would you tell me, please, which way I ought to go from here?"
"That depends on a good deal on where you want to get to," said the Cat.
"I don't much care where–" said Alice.
"Then it doesn't matter which way you go," said the Cat.
"–so long as I get SOMEWHERE," Alice added as an explanation.
"Oh, you're sure to do that," said the Cat, "if you only walk long enough." –
(ALICE'S ADVENTURES IN WONDERLAND)

As a child, I never understood Alice in Wonderland. It was filled with weird scenes and a terrifying Queen that was not very nice. Today, I still don't know if I fully understand every symbolism that the book portrays. I do however get what the Cheshire Cat was trying to say to Alice in the quote above.

If you don't know where you want to go, then any path will get you there. In the same way, if you don't take the time to Plan, you risk finding yourself moving away from your goals.

If you are serious about increasing your productivity, then make planning a habit.

Do you plan your day in advance? If not, chances are that very often, you find yourself in reaction mode instead of following up on your strategies. With proper planning, you can be proactive and clear about what you want to accomplish each day.

Which planning habits can you put in place that will help increase your productivity?

The following steps can help you create the right planning habits:

Step 1: First be effective, then efficient

Before you can even begin to be productive, you need to determine what productive means to you. No, it is not the number of tasks you get done in a day. In fact, sometimes only getting 1-2 things done can be more productive than another day where you get 30 menial tasks done.

- ✓ Determine your Most Important Tasks for the Day. What are the 1-2 Big Rocks that need to be done that will advance you towards your goals fastest?
- ✓ Know what outcome you want to achieve from your day.
- ✓ Capture everything you need to do (paper or electronic).

Step 2: Now be Efficient

Now that you know what you need to be effective, schedule your day to be most efficient.

- ✓ Make sure all your Deadlines and Appointments are scheduled into your calendar.
- ✓ Next, schedule your Big Rocks and Most Important Tasks according to your energy levels. When is your energy highest? These are the moments to work on those tasks that require the most energy from you.
- ✓ Batch similar tasks together. This allows for a minimum

transition from one task to another.
- ✓ Try theming your days for maximum efficiency. If possible, try and schedule your meetings all on one day. Have your development discussions or 1-1 on the same day every week.
- ✓ Leave Open Blocks for the unexpected. These will be the moments where you can manage the urgent without it impacting what is important.
- ✓ Schedule time to read emails or return messages.

Note on multi-tasking: Although the ability to multi-task has once been revered, it has now been proven that it hinders your productivity instead of increasing it. Dr. Sanjay Gupta, Chief Medical Correspondent for CNN, mentioned that there is only about 2% of the population that are super multitaskers. It's a genetic gift. In fact, most of us don't have this gift. These are the people who are truly able to do several different activities at the same time without losing efficiency or losing quality as they do all that work.

According to Dr. Sanjay's research, while you may think you are multitasking, you're not doing both activities at the same time. What you are doing is diverting your attention from one part of your brain to another part of your brain. That takes time, resources and brain cells. What happens on the other side of the brain is that you're starting a brand new activity, so in fact, you're probably slower and not nearly as good at doing both activities at the same time.

Based on these findings, I recommend single tasking items that are high level. These are those tasks that are part of your Big Rocks (Most Important Tasks) and would benefit from your undivided attention. You can then multitask low level, more menial items.

How do you determine what your Most Important Tasks are? These are based on your values and priority goals that you set for yourself during Part 1 of this book, dealing with Mindset. Your MIT tasks are those 20% that will bring you closest to your main goals.

Step 3: Mid-Day Check-in

Checking on your progress midday is important. This will allow you to gauge if you are on track to accomplishing all you intended to complete. Are your Most Important Tasks done? Make sure to adjust your afternoon if necessary based on your results so far.

Step 4: Review. Plan. Repeat

Another check-in? Your midday check-in was to ensure you were going to be able to complete those tasks you deemed a priority and to realign if necessary. This step is about reviewing your entire day and taking note of anything important.

At the Beginning of the process, don't get discouraged if you over plan too much. The key is to learn from what didn't work during the day and to continue doing more of what did work.

The end of day review is also about creating your plan for the next day based on the events of the current day and what you foresee as your priorities for the next day.

Review. Plan. Repeat

PART III: RIGHT SYSTEMS

CHAPTER TEN – Finding Planning Systems That Work For You

> *" The European myth that arose of El Dorado, as a lost city of gold waiting for discovery by an adventurous conqueror, encapsulates the Europeans' endless thirst for gold and their unerring drive to exploit these new lands for their monetary value."*

There is a legend of a vast city called El Dorado that contained unimaginable mineral riches. A city of gold. Europeans of the sixteenth century believed so much in this city, that several Spanish conquistadors often made perilous, deadly journeys to find it. But in spite of such valiant efforts, El Dorado seems to persist only as a symbol of the rapacious greed with which the English and Spanish beheld the New World. It has now become synonymous with a place of fabulous wealth or inordinately great opportunity.

My search for the right productivity strategy felt much the same way. O.K, a little exaggeration to make a point. I did, however, feel several times that finding the right productivity system was a legend that was not meant for me to achieve.

As I wrote at the beginning of the book, I have tried all types of productivity systems. I was determined to find the right one for me. Most of them worked for a while but never sustained my interest. I even spent quite a bit of money to find and buy the system that would magically make me "productive." I was intent on finding the right software. I tried most of the newest and most popular productivity systems. Nothing worked. I would get excited when one seemed to work well, then realize not too long after that it wouldn't stick. Some did a good job tracking what I needed to get done but were of no use if I never used it. It was an on and off relationship that drove me nuts.

I was beginning to lose all hope. Until I implemented the practices taught in this book.

I needed to start with the right mindset. It wasn't about making the most popular productivity system work for me. It didn't even need to be complicated. It just needed to be one that I could integrate best with my habits. The system that I can quickly make subconscious.

When I stopped focusing on the system but my mindset and habits instead, I started gaining traction. My advice is pick something that works for you. I realized that all those available productivity apps were not where I needed to start. I needed to start with me.

- How do I think, prioritize and organize my time?
- When did I feel most productive? What about that time worked?

"The best productivity system is one that makes your productivity flow, not obstruct it."

What I want to emphasize is that there is no one size fits all system. It simply does not exist. We are all very different and what motivates one person does not always motivate another. So don't worry about picking the "best productivity app," or the most expensive productivity app. Try a few but stick with the one that works for you.

To learn which productivity system works for you, test and move on when needed. Don't stay stuck determined to make one system work for you.

Here are 11 Steps for Choosing a Good Productivity System:

1. You don't have to stick to one productivity method forever. You may find a method that works well for some projects but not others. It may suit your style one year but not another. Be flexible and don't be afraid to make a change.
2. The goal is not to get the most stuff done but get the right things done. It is actually about doing less in order to accomplish more.
3. Sometimes simple is better.
4. The right system should automate and schedule.
5. The best systems are friction-free – it should be easy to put tasks in, organize them and see what needs to be done next.
6. The right system for you should be easily adaptable to how you want to work.
7. Pick a system that is easy to learn.
8. As the world gets more interconnected, a good productivity system should make it easy to collaborate with others.
9. Choose a system that is compatible with other systems.
10. In order to make the best use of your system, it should be one that is easily portable, and you can take with you at all times.
11. Avoid having too many tools for particular tasks. Have one system for calendars, to-do lists, and notebooks.

Before we delve into the main productivity systems available for you, let me make an important point. Busyness can be a drug. I use to purposely write down as many things down on my task list just so that I can "check them off" the list. The measure of my productivity was based on the number of tasks I was able to tick off my list. There was no differentiation between what was important or unimportant.

Sometimes, being constantly busy might even be seen as a status symbol.

Busy = Important

You hear it all the time. "I am so busy. So much to do." As if this meant that being busy was a good thing. The mindset I am suggesting is that you replace busy with productive. Out of all the busy tasks, you need to accomplish, how many directly impact the achievement of your most important goals?

In the next few chapters, I will review the current most popular productivity systems as well as some productivity apps available for you at the time of writing this book.

CHAPTER ELEVEN – 7 Effective Productivity Systems

" The perfect is the enemy of the good." — Voltaire

I started this chapter with a great quote from Voltaire. "The perfect is the enemy of the good." Aiming for perfection slows down progress. How many times did you or someone you know wait for something to be perfect before committing to a project? I have done this so many times myself. It can be hard to ignore a flaw when you see one. The truth is, nothing is perfect.

No productivity system will adapt to your needs perfectly. Find the one that works best with your lifestyle and your habits. Don't focus on the perfect system. It does not exist.

So how do you know where to start finding the perfect productivity system? This chapter will cover five of the most popular productivity systems that are around. Read through the chapter and start with what connects with you first and start from there. I would even recommend a mix of different productivity systems. Take a tool from each system if needed. There are no rules.

After this chapter, we will then review the different productivity apps that are available. These can be used as a standalone app or in conjunction with another system. Then I will tackle one of the biggest deterrents to your productivity, emails. If you don't have an effective way to manage your email, it can be a big time waster and energy drainer. I will review a simple yet effective system.

1. Stephen Covey's Time Matrix and Productivity Pyramid

Stephen Covey's book, "7 Habits of Highly Effective People," was the first personal development book that I read. I was 16 years old when I first read it, and I still have the original book that is earmarked, highlighted, read and re-read several times. If you haven't read the book yet, it is a must read. It is not just about productivity but about building habits that can have a major positive impact in your lives. The strategies I learned at 16, I still use today.

The book covers two important topics when we talk about increasing productivity, "The Time Matrix" and "The Productivity Matrix."

The Time Matrix:

We live in a world of multiple overlapping commitments. Several things are vying for our attention, and most of them require immediate attention now. Urgency is no longer reserved for unique situations. They are everyday occurrences.

Stephen Covey talks about how we spend our time in one of four ways, which he called Quadrants.

The two factors that define an activity are urgent and important. Urgent means it requires immediate attention. It's "Now." A good example is someone walking into your office and asking for your time. You cannot just ignore them. You need to act, even if it is to ask them to come back at a later predesignated time. Urgent matters are usually visible and insist on action.

Important, on the other hand, has to do with results. If something is important, it contributes to your mission, your values, your high priority goals. Important matters that are not urgent require more initiative, more proactivity.

The Quadrants are broken down as follows:

Stephen Covey's Time Management Matrix

	URGENT	NOT URGENT
IMPORTANT	Quadrant I: Urgent & Important	Quadrant II: Not Urgent & Important
NOT IMPORTANT	Quadrant III: Urgent & Not Important	Quadrant IV: Not Urgent & Not Important

Quadrant I: for immediate and important deadlines.
Quadrant II: For long-term strategizing and development.
Quadrant III: For time pressured distractions. Not important to your mission, values or goals, but someone wants it now.
Quadrant IV: For activities that yield little value.

Sometimes, because an activity falls in the urgent, you may think it is important. The reality is that the urgency of these matters is often based on the priorities and expectations of others.

Productive people work very hard to build on their Quadrant II activities. This is at the heart of effective personal management. It deals with things that are not urgent, but important. Activities in this quadrant include building relationships, long-range planning, exercising, goal setting, people development and all those things we need to do but put on the back burner. It is easy to put off doing these activities because the "urgent" takes over. However, investing in this Quadrant will bring you the biggest ROI.

Throughout my career, I saw many managers fall into this trap. They let the urgent take control and don't spend enough time on the important. I've often had conversations with them questioning what they have done to develop their team. Too often, "I don't have time for one on ones or development meetings" is the answer I hear. Unfortunately, a disengaged workforce creates more workload after. Investing in your people is a Quadrant II activity. Dealing with the urgencies that arise in a disengaged workforce are Quadrant III activities.

The Productivity Pyramid:
Another concept from Stephen Covey is the Productivity Pyramid. Imagine a Pyramid with four levels. At the bottom of the pyramid are your values. It always starts with your values.! What is important to you? It is in defining first what is important to you that determines your most important goals.

The second level of the pyramid is your goals. Now that you know what you value and what is most important, you can determine what goals you need to accomplish in order to achieve more of what you value. There are many resources available today that help you delve into best practices for Goal Setting. Like productivity systems, don't make your goal-setting complicated.

Here are simple Goal-Setting Tips

1. Write it down.
2. Give it a deadline.
3. Break it down into doable chunks.
4. Commit.

Tip 3 and 4 are what the last two levels of the productivity pyramid are about. Ideally, you have set a stretch goal that takes more effort to accomplish it. A goal that will challenge but can be achieved. You now have that Bulls-Eye target at your site. What you need to plan are the steps it will take to get you from where you are to where you need to go to hit the target.

Step 3 of the pyramid is to Plan your weekly goals. These are the small, doable chunks from Tip 3. What steps need to be taken weekly to move you towards your goal.

Finally, what does that look like daily? Plan the daily tasks that need to be accomplished to achieve your big goal.

Putting it together:

By combining the Time Matrix and Productivity Pyramid together, we get Covey's Productivity system. You are setting your goals and breaking it down; you will be focusing on your Quadrant II goals. Plan it on your calendar and make sure you do important things first.

2. The Eisenhower Matrix

The Eisenhower Matrix is similar to Covey's Time Management matrix. If I had to guess, it would be that Covey got his inspiration from Eisenhower. I still put it as a separate productivity system for your review. The difference in both systems is in the name of each Quadrant. Pick your preference of what works for you.

Dwight D. Eisenhower was the 24th President of the United States from 1953 until 1961. Before he became President, he served as a general in the United States Army. He also became NATO's first supreme commander. As a general, supreme commander and then President, Dwight had to make tough decisions every day. He could not afford to invest time in tasks that were not important. In order to guide his decision making, he invented the Eisenhower Matrix, a principle-centered productivity system around prioritizing the urgent and important.

One of the main advantages of the Eisenhower Matrix is that it helps you determine which tasks you should put on your to-do list and which tasks you should delegate or eliminate.

If you already have a to-do list, take a few moments to read it over. Where does your task fall under the Matrix? Proper time management takes practice and today is a good time to start.

Do First	Schedule
First focus on important tasks to be done the same day	Important, but not so-urgent tasks should be scheduled
Delegate	**Don't Do**
Tasks that are urgent, but less important, delegate	What's neither urgent nor important, remove from task list completely

As you can see, although it is similar to the Time Management Matrix, Eisenhower's is more about the actions you should do in each Quadrant.

Tips when working with the Eisenhower Matrix:
- Create a to-do list similar to the Eisenhower Matrix
- Start putting tasks that need to be accomplished according to the Quadrant they belong to.

- Try limiting yourself to no more than eight tasks per quadrant before adding another one.
- Always complete the most important task first. It is not about a number of tasks you complete but the number of tasks that lead to your most important goals.
- It is great practice to maintain a separate list for both business and personal tasks. This ensures that you keep focusing on every important area of your life.
- Never let others define your priority. Plan the night before or early in the morning.

"What is important is seldom urgent, and what is urgent is seldom important." Dwight Eisenhower

3. David Allen's Getting Things Done Methodology

Getting Things Done, or "GTD" as it's more commonly known, is not only a productivity system but also a movement. The concept was created by David Allen, a management consultant as a way to help executives manage the daily tasks of running a business. Since its creation, it has been refined and is probably one of the most used productivity systems today.

Simply put, GTD is a method for organizing your to-dos, priorities and your schedule into a manageable chunk. One of its main benefits is the ease of seeing all your responsibilities on one plate and making it clear what to do next. GTD also has a reputation for being complicated although it doesn't have to be. Remember, the rule in the beginning of this chapter? There are no rules. Adapt any system to what works for you.

The whole concept of GTD is five simple steps that are meant to provide you structure and allow you to be more creative, strategic and focused.

GTD Methodology:

CAPTURE: Collect what has your attention

Have a tool or tools for collecting all your ideas, recurring tasks, projects and everything that needs to be handled or finished. There is no specific tool required just use what fits best in your normal flow. It should be something that you can access quickly so you can capture everything as soon as it happens. It should also be flexible, so if a new task or project arises, you can get it out of your head and into your system as quickly as possible. If your current to-do app does not allow this freedom, find one that does. The idea of capturing everything is that it clears your mind of any mental distractions that will keep you from working efficiently.

CLARIFY: Process what it means

Once you have captured everything that is necessary, ask yourself one simple question, "Is it actionable?" If the answer is "No," then trash it, or file it as a reference. If "Yes," then decide on the very next action required. An important tip emphasized in the GTD book is the two-minute rule. Anything that takes less than two minutes to accomplish should be done right away. It takes longer to defer it or put it on a calendar than accomplishing the task immediately. The rest goes on a task list or calendar for processing later.

ORGANIZE: Put it where it belongs

Break down larger projects into smaller, actionable steps.
Anything that has a due date should be placed on a calendar.
Create lists for appropriate categories i.e. emails to send, calls to make, meetings, etc...

REFLECT: Review frequently

This is probably one of the most important steps but a step that frequently gets skipped. Set aside some reflection time to review your task list. There is no faster way to waste time on work than working blindly without relooking at the big picture to see if you are still heading in the right direction. I recommend reviewing your list at the beginning of each day to ensure you start with your most important priorities. A quick review at the end will help you review your productive day.

If reviewing the list twice in one day is too much, then consider a daily beginning review and a complete end of week review. Evaluate what got accomplished and plan out your next week's priorities and tasks.

By separating the tasks into separate categories, you will be able to quickly see what's important, what takes the most or least time to accomplish and what you need to tackle next.

ENGAGE: Simple do.

Continue to capture, clarify, organize and reflect on an ongoing basis until it becomes a natural part of your productivity system.

The GTD system can take some discipline and time to learn it properly and use regularly. It is not a good system for people who can't commit to its guidelines or don't have the discipline to get the most out of the system.

4. Kanban System

The Kanban system, formulated by David J. Anderson, is a work scheduling system intended to maximize the productivity of a team by reducing idle time. Software development teams and IT project managers widely make use of Kanban boards. However, it can be used for personal task management. Trello app is an excellent example of an app designed for Kanban.

The bottom line is that Personal Kanban keeps all your to-dos in front of you and prioritized, so you never wonder what to work on next. Some are complicated, but others make it easy to see everything, organized by priority. Kanban is similar to GTD in the combining and prioritizing of tasks.

Basic concepts:
- Kanban is based on the idea of boards, lists, and cards.
- Each board represents an overall area or project (starting a blog, creating a CRM network, etc.).
- A board normally has several lists on it.
- Each list represents a distinct part of the lifecycle of that project (To Do, In Progress, In Testing, Done).
- A list has several cards on it.
- Each card represents a specific action (i.e. choosing a platform for your blog, choosing your blog theme).

Advantages of using Kanban:
- Reduction of wasted work
- Ability to visibly see all tasks and projects
- Team members know where each step of the project is at
- Increased productivity
- Increased efficiency
- Flexibility

How to use Kanban to Improve Productivity:

Step 1: Visualize the work

All you need is a spot where you can lay out and arrange your to-dos into a Kanban Board. Kanban boards can be a traditional whiteboard, a simple board with three or four vertical columns, or an online software-based Kanban. More on online-based Kanban later.

Break down the workflow of each project or task into clear-cut steps. A simple step process that can be applied to various projects and tasks are; To Do, Doing, On Hold, Done.

For each of the steps, draw a column. Once this is done, obtain some stickies. Note down all tasks, separating a sticky note for each. You can use different coloured notes for each project.

Step 2: Limits

The advantage of a board is that it allows you to quickly determine if you are prioritizing too many tasks and projects at one. Start imposing limits on the columns where tasks are being done. This will ensure that you focus on the few that will bring the greatest results.

Step 3: Pull

Kanban is considered a pull system. Work items are pulled into the queue by the people doing the work as they complete tasks in order of priority. Kanban enables you to focus on the Minimum Viable Product (MVP) or as it is sometimes referred to, Minimum Marketable Features (MFF).

MVP is a term that was popularized by two Silicon Valley Entrepreneurs, Eric Ries and Steve Blank. Simply put, a Minimum Viable Product is that version of a new product which allows a team to collect the maximum amount of validated learning about customers with the least effort.

Translated to personal productivity, Kanban allows you to quickly determine if the task or project you are working on will bring you towards your desired goal.

Step 4: Reflection

I am sure you are starting to notice a similar pattern in all productivity systems. Take the time to evaluate your progress and ensure that the system you are using is maximizing your productivity.

"The best measure of any system is first to give it a chance for measurement and second to be consistent in its use." -Elita Torres

Apps and Tools for Kanban:

If you don't have the space for a huge whiteboard in your living space or a smaller desk pad version, there are other options available to you.

Here are 5 Kanban Tools that can be adapted for a personal productivity system.

1. **Trello: (Trello.com)** This extremely popular productivity tool is built around Kanban-style task organization. They have boards, lists, and cards available for you to organize and prioritize your projects. All you need to do is define your columns and start adding to-dos.

2. **KanbanFlow: (Kanbanflow.com)** This tool was designed clearly with the Kanban approach. KanbanFlow offers a customizable workflow and columns to fit your preferred way of working. Some of the great features available with this tool are: adding notes and reminders to items, adding subtasks, adding recurring tasks, ability to limit your work in progress, collaborate with others and the ability to integrate a Pomodoro Timer. It is worth taking a look at their site, and no app is required.

3. **Kanban Tool: (Kanbantool.com)** Kanban Tool allows you to visualize your workflow, analyse and improve business processes in line with the Kanban method. They have a paid monthly membership, but you can start for free with a personal account.

4. **Kanbanize: (Kanbanize.com)** Kanbanize offers an end-to-end platform for managing, executing, and even analysing your workflow, helping you find bottlenecks and remove them from the system - one by one. It does come with a 30-day trial period, but then you need to choose a monthly plan. Therefore, I would only recommend this if you are working on a team project since there are great alternate free tools available for personal use.

5. **Evernote (Evernote.com)** with **Kanbanote (Kanbanote.com)** Evernote is a great software for managing notes and tasks but doesn't have a Kanban view of notes. Kanbanote is optimized for Getting Things Done (GTD) with Kanban methodology. It

adds the three Backlog/Doing/Done columns for you with an available companion Android app as well.

Scrum framework:

Jeff Sutherland co-created an approach called "Scrum" and wrote a book detailing the process, "Scrum: The Art of Doing Twice the Work in Half the Time." The goal of Scrum was to create an agile framework for accomplishing complex projects. It was originally formalized for software development projects but works well for any complex, innovative scope of work.

Basic concepts:

- A product owner creates a prioritized wish list called a product backlog.
- A team has a certain amount of time – a sprint (usually two to four weeks) – to complete its work but meets each day to assess its progress (daily Scrum).
- During sprint planning, the team pulls a small chunk from the top of the wish list and decides how to implement those pieces.
- The Scrum Master keeps the team focused on its goal.
- The sprint ends with a sprint review and retrospective.
- As the next sprint begins, the team chooses another chunk of the product backlog and begins working again
- During sprints, you periodically stop your work and determine if it's still what you should be doing and how you might be doing it better.

The Scrum methodology has a lot of similar features to the Kanban methodology and can be used in conjunction with your productivity process. As a Sales Director where I work, we are currently using Scrum for reshaping our brand. It is early in the process, but the feedback has been extremely positive. You can find whiteboards in almost every conference room plastered with Kanban style tasks.

If you are considering Kanban, a look into Scrum may be beneficial.

The Scrum book is also a great read with great productivity insights for project management.

5. Don't Break the Chain

The next two productivity systems are more about building habits but are considered productivity systems. This is a very simple productivity system that helps you build momentum. Sometimes the simplest systems are the most powerful.

So many of us start something, then because we don't see immediate results, we grow impatient and give up. When I learned about momentum in physics, I was taught that momentum was a mass in motion. What I learned throughout my career was that the power of momentum came from the force.

Momentum is not a one-time thing. It takes time. The good news is that the force does not have to be massive to achieve results. A small force applied over and over again can build enough momentum to result in a powerful habit.

Some examples of how momentum can be applied:
- A 1000 kg car moving at 15 m/sec has a momentum of 15,000 kg/sec as a result of multiplying the mass and the velocity.
- A karate expert can generate enough speed with his fist that the momentum can carry through several bricks breaking them.
- If you have ever been sledding, you know that at the top of the hill you may have to push a little to build momentum. As you start sliding down a snowy hill, your sled builds momentum and its speed increases, without any more effort on your part.

Don't Break the Chain helps you create the momentum you need to build that habit.

Remember the Productivity equation:

Productivity Equation = Right Mindset + **Right Habits** + Right Systems + Your Plan

Once you have built enough momentum, a habit takes form. Once the habit is formed, the amount of energy required to accomplish the task greatly reduces. The key is in building consistency.

Don't Break the Chain is a system that was used by Jerry Seinfeld in an attempt to make him a better comic. He knew that in order to write better jokes, he needed to write every day. In order to motivate himself into making daily writing a habit, he created his productivity system.

Basic concepts:
- Decide on one thing you want to improve over time (writing, exercising, eating a healthy meal or any habit you want to build).
- Get a big wall calendar or an online calendar app.
- Next, get a big red magic marker.
- Every day, do something towards building your habit or your long-term goal.
- Put a big red X in the calendar box if you completed your task for that day.
- After a few days, a chain is created.
- Keep the chain of X's going for as long as possible.

The concept is simple. It is based on the idea that as the chain grows, you won't want to break it. It works because it isn't a sometimes push that gets you where you want to go. It is the consistent daily action that builds momentum and creates extraordinary outcomes.

Daily action builds habits. It allows for practice and allows you to become an expert in a short time. Your goal is not to break the chain or skip a day because skipping one day makes it easier to skip the next. Those fries one day make it easier to eat the donut the next day.

An important note is that this productivity system is not meant as a task management, project planning or as a traditional to-do list technique.

You can still use it to complete a project by setting daily actions you need to accomplish towards your project. Once you have determined a daily action, you can use, "Don't Break the Chain" method to build momentum and help you accomplish that project.

I used this method to develop a daily habit of writing every day. I was having difficulty managing my career as a Sales Director, writing posts for my blog and working on this book. I would come home at the end of a long day and find myself lacking the energy to write. I waited until the weekend to do most of my writing but the majority of my available time was spent on keeping my **www.LeadGrowDevelop.com** blog current. I aimed for a goal of writing every day and used the, "Don't Break the Chain Method" to build my writing habit.

My first attempt, I managed only two Red X's. Then, 5 and I slowly built momentum from there.

Take a moment to reflect on what action you can take that would make the biggest impact on your productivity, or life if you worked on it every day. That is the action that I would recommend you put on your productivity calendar. What will be your first big X? Then, make sure that you …

"Don't Break the Chain"

6. The Pomodoro Technique

When I used to have a large project that I needed to work on, I used to force myself to spend countless hours concentrating on the same task. I was naïve in thinking that the more hours I put in, the more productivity I would have.

Similar to my College and University years, I tried to cram all my work into long sessions. It was easier then. There weren't as many distractions available as there are now. Back then, I didn't even own a computer, not to mention a smartphone nor IPad. With social media and the constant pinging of notifications, staying focused for long periods of time can be a challenge.

Do you find that your productivity fluctuates depending on the day? Some days you accomplish every task on your list. While other days you find yourself "surfing for ideas" but not really getting anywhere.

Productivity is not a time allotted concept. It is an alignment between a progression towards your goals and the discipline to keep building those habits to keep you moving forward.

A 2008 University of Illinois study showed that being tethered to your desk for long periods of time actually reduces your productivity. In contrast, taking regular short breaks help to keep you focused and energized.

During his first year of university, Francesco Cirillo quickly realized that "cramming" was not helping him with his studies. He found himself getting distracted and not making use of his study time efficiently. To combat this, he grabbed a tomato-shaped kitchen timer, set it for 10 minutes, and tried to work solidly for those 10 minutes without doing anything else. Francesco found that this method worked for him and he even rewarded himself with a break.

He continued to test and tweak this method and Cirillo settled on a structured framework that he called the Pomodoro Technique. Pomodoro, the Italian word for "tomato" was a reference to his original kitchen timer.

Basic concepts:
- Get a timer
- Decide on a task you want to work on
- Set your timer for 20-25 minutes
- During that time, work on the task and nothing else. Close any apps or eliminate any possible distractions.

- At the end of that time, take a short five-minute break. Stand up, stretch, drink water or do anything that can refresh you. Stay away from anything that will tempt you into taking a longer short break.
- You've just completed your first Pomodoro.
- After your short break set your timer again for another 20-25 minutes.
- Once you've completed four Pomodoros in a row, take a longer 20-minute break.

Pomodoro is a cyclical system. It encourages you to work in short, focused sprints. The regular breaks help keep your energy levels high and bolster your motivation. Highly focused work sessions help you manage your time more effectively and makes large projects seem less overwhelming.

When there is something that you know you need to do but are just not motivated to do it, try committing to a small goal first. If you know that housework needs to be done but are finding it difficult to start, commit to just 15 minutes of housework to start. Often, I use this self-motivating starter method to begin a task I have been procrastinating on. What I quickly discover is that once I start the task, I am able to keep going beyond the original time commitment.

Pomodoro works in a similar fashion. It allows you to break a large task into smaller focused tasks to maintain high energy levels and increased productivity. However, the method may not suit everyone. Some people might find regular short breaks too distracting, especially during times when inspiration is flowing. It might also be difficult to stick to a disciplined schedule of Pomodoro depending on your work environment.

The important thing to remember is the goal of keeping your energy levels high and maintaining your focus on a single task at hand to increase productivity. You can adapt the work periods and break periods to suit what works best for you. Listen to your body. If your mind starts to wander, or if you start feeling tired, don't push through to the end of the session.

Our body rhythms naturally flow from 90 to 120-minute cycles, and it is difficult to know at what stage of your ultradian rhythm you were at when you began your task. The ultradian rhythm is a cycle that's present in both our sleeping and waking lives. Nathan Kleitman, a groundbreaking sleep researcher, was the first to discover this "basic rest-activity cycle." You probably heard of the 90-minute cycle during which you progress through the five stages of sleep. What Kleitman found was that this 90-minute pattern was present in our days too. We move from higher to lower alertness – the ultradian rhythm.

I recommend that you experiment with what works for you. It may be three Pomodoros followed by a 10-minute break, or three sessions of 30 minutes with a 5-minute break in-between. There are no set rules. You decide what works for you.

There are also several apps available to help you with this technique. I will review a few on a later chapter.

The Pomodoro Experiment

When I first started the Pomodoro method, I found that I was deep into flow when the timer would go off. 25 Minutes didn't work well for me. At first, I would force myself to follow the system the way it was meant to be. 25 minutes, followed by a 5-minute break and repeat. I would still find myself wanting some extra time.

Then, I realized that I should be a little more flexible and that I needed to adapt the system to me and not the other way around.

So I started testing the time. I started with doubling it but found it difficult to be "in the zone" for that long. I decreased and increased the time until I found one that worked.

Currently, I have a 37-minute Focus time and 13-minute refresh time. 40 minutes was too long, and 37 just worked. When I write on the weekends where I have more free time, I try 2 Pomodoros in a row before I can check off my writing for the day. During the week, where my Director job and kids' homework take up the majority of my day and early evening, I commit to at least one session only.

If there is a night where I feel exhausted, I commit to at least a 25 min. Pomodoro. Normally, I find myself able to continue to 37 minutes.

7. The Good Old "To-do List" Productivity System

Start by doing what's necessary; then do what's possible, and suddenly you are doing the impossible. – Francis of Assisi

Continuing on the power of simplicity comes the well-known to do list. No matter which new productivity system I tried, I often found myself going back to the good old task list. There is that "instant gratification" feel good injection when you tick something off a list. It is also a great tool to keep all your to-do's organized, so you don't miss a project.

Note: Your Outlook or email is not meant for a to-do list. The option to flag an email as a reminder is meant for filing purposes or for quick reference but not a good option to keep all your tasks and projects organized.

The to-do list isn't as effective for multi-step projects, more complex tasks, or for organizing lots of different tasks at once. It is, however, a great tool for prioritizing if you follow the basic concepts:

Tips for To-Do list Mastery: It is not about quantity but quality. The items on your to-do list should be priority tasks that need to get done. Change the name of To-Do to Must-Do. You can use the Eisenhower Matrix as a guide for what you should be putting on your to-do list.

Best Practices:
- Decide on your to-do list vehicle; paper, computer or app. It really is about what works best for you.
- Keep it simple.
- Prep your to-do list the night before. Have your first three tasks numbered in order of priority so you can begin your day with your Must Do tasks.
- Start with your overall to-do list or collection of tasks you need to get done.
- Focus on what you absolutely must get done **today.** What actions can you take that will move your business forward?
- Set up recurring tasks to save time on re-entering tasks on a regular basis. If you are a pen and paper person, recurring tasks can be written then photocopied, so you don't have to rewrite it.
- Once you have completed the first three priority tasks, determine your next two priority tasks.
- Don't put more tasks then you can accomplish in one day.
- Appointments are not a task and should instead be scheduled on your calendar. The preparation needed for an appointment, however, can be a task.
- You can set reminders on tasks that need to be accomplished based on the order you want to accomplish them.

Be strategic when you are creating your to-do list. If you have a list of over 50 tasks that need to be accomplished, then you need to revisit your priorities. Focus only on your Most Important Tasks for that day.

CHAPTER TWELVE - Productivity Apps to Get You Started

"Infinite striving to be the best is man's duty; It is its own reward. Everything else is in God's hands.." – Mahatma Gandhi

This chapter is all about giving you some choices of tools you can use to build your productivity system. If plain old pen and paper are not enough for you, then this chapter will give you a variety of Productivity Apps you can choose from.

Think of it as a reference chapter or an experiment chapter where you can have fun trying a variety of apps. I have broken it down by category for easy reference. Depending on what you are looking to systematize, you can start from there.

This is only a small percentage of what is available. I recommend that you don't get too caught up in trying them all. You can get lost in all the details, and the search for the right productivity app may become a deterrent to your productivity. So where do you begin? Match a productivity app with your style of task management.

How do you go about managing your to-do's? Do you group them in a certain way? Are you in need of extra details, or do you keep task descriptions short? Are you more visual and want to measure progress?

Your answers to these questions will help you in deciding which task management method works best for you. If you do fine with a simple to-do list, then look for a grocery list style app. Do you need more flexibility from your system, then try a GTD style app. More visual? Try a Kanban board app.

Other factors to take into account are the ability to integrate cross-platform (mobile, web, and desktop), the ability to share tasks if that is what you need and its ease of use. Another important feature of a productivity app is the ability to integrate with your calendar.

Some apps can be found in more than one category. A task management app can be used as a note-taking app or a calendar app. The way they are categorized is based on their main functionality.

This list although extensive is only a small portion of what is available. Do your research and test. The remaining chapter only highlights what is available as options at the time of this writing.

Task Management Apps

Any.do (Android, iOS, The Web, Free or Premium version)

One of the more popular apps, Any.do is there to keep your schedule on track with to-do list, reminders, notes and the ability to share lists with and assign tasks to others. It even has a voice-entry feature for ease of use. A voice-entry feature allows you to add items to your task list just by speaking.

Calendar integration is available for better task list management. Further enhance your productivity with cross-platform support for sub-tasks, notes, and file attachments.

http://www.any.do/

Wunderlist (Android, iOS, Web, Free or Premium version)

The beauty of Wunderlist is in its simplicity. It gives the user the choice to create a bunch of list groupings (think GTD) and under each of those groupings, a list of tasks. You can have as many contexts as you want and as many tasks in each context as you want. Your tasks can have a due date, reminder, a note, or a star.

The ability to sync to all of your other devices is a bonus. Your list is organized by categories, and you can even add new tasks by sending yourself an email.

https://www.wunderlist.com/

Remember the Milk (Android, iOS, Web, Free or Premium version)

This productivity app has a large following. In addition to allowing you to set time limits, locations, and automatic updates when a task is finished, this app is very user-friendly. It also allows you to share tasks with others.

Other great features are its Search Wizard that allows you to quickly find a task and Smart Add. Smart Add allows you to quickly create a task by typing. For example, by entering "Review sales reports weekly

Monday at 8 a.m", the app will create a recurring task for Mondays at 8 a.m.

The app also allows syncing to Gmail, Google Calendar, Twitter, Evernote, and Outlook.

https://www.rememberthemilk.com/

Checkmark 2 (iOS)

This app is more of a reminder app than a complete task management app. When you are within a certain radius of a new location (home, work, grocery store, etc.), that venue's to-do list will pop up, reminding you right away what you need to do. You simply name your locations and the reminders based on location. Example, you can set a reminder to buy milk every time you are at the grocery store.

Want to impress your spouse or partner? Set a reminder to ask them about their day every time you arrive at home. Corny? Maybe. Effective? It can be.

Toodledo (Android, iOS, Web, Free)

Toodledo has been around for a while and continues to be extremely popular. It is one of the best web apps for keeping track of your tasks and projects with an incredible number of features. It has also been featured on many top GTD and productivity app lists.

Some of its task management features are; creating folders and subtasks, prioritizing tasks, creating tags and starring tasks. It also has a hotlist and the ability to create goals. Toodledo comes with a calendar and time tracking function and gives you the ability to collaborate on tasks. A popular feature as well is a habit tracker allowing you to track and build great habits.

Toodledo has the ability to connect to many popular services and devices to allow you to access your tasks from anywhere. There are more than 50 third-party apps and tools that are built upon their free and open developers API.

The app has data visualization that allows you to create and customize graphs and charts to see an overview of your productivity.

https://www.toodledo.com/

Todoist (Android, iOS, The Web, Free with Premium option available)

If you're looking for a to-do list app that works on all your devices, has great features for monitoring your productivity, and gives you several options on the organization of tasks, Todoist is for you. This app allows you to break tasks down into sub-tasks and also see an overview of your week, with larger more pressing tasks highlighted. Plug-ins are available for most web browsers and Outlook email.

It also has a data visualization feature and gives you Karma points based on user set preferences that measure your productivity.

This is the app I use. I have tried several others but enjoyed this one the most. Nothing really magical about it that other apps don't have it just spoke to me the most. Remember that is the idea. Finding a task management app that works for you and not necessarily the one that is most popular. I have paid the $29/year fee for the premium option, but it is not a must. I love the #"name of project" feature to quickly add tasks to projects. The app also has a smart add function where I can quickly add recurring tasks and set deadlines. I currently have several projects created for work as well as projects for personal use and my LeadGrowDevelop.com brand.

Asana (Android, iOS, The Web, Free with Upgradeable options)

Asana was created by former Facebook co-founder Dustin Moskovitz and former Facebook employee, Justin Rosenstein. It allows you to create Workspaces – which are really more than projects. You can even create projects inside of Workspaces.

Workspaces essentially are, "areas of focus" that you need to keep organized. They have several layers to them so you can manage tasks and projects within them. Projects are the backbone of Asana, as opposed to tasks in other systems of note.

Think of Asana as a digital Kanban system for team projects. With tasks, projects, conversations, and dashboards, it allows teams to move work from start to finish.

https://asana.com/

Trello (Android, iOS, Web, Slack, Free with Upgradeable options)
Trello is a great Kanban system or Scrum system that helps you work more collaboratively with your team and get more done. Trello's boards, lists, and cards enable you to organize and prioritize projects in a flexible and rewarding way. You can also integrate the apps that your team already uses directly into your workflow. Power-Ups turn Trello boards into living applications.

If you are visual, it could be a great tool to keep you organized and see all the steps in the workflow in one place. There is even a Gmail Chrome Extension that allows you to quickly add an email to a list on a board.

Integrating Trello with Productivity Systems:

Trello can be used in conjunction with some of the productivity systems mentioned in the previous chapter.

Kanban: Kanban is a system that organizes workflow visually, often with cards organized into columns (such as "To Do," "Doing," and "Done"). Trello gets its inspiration from the Kanban board and is a great way of managing projects.

As an example, imagine that you work for the HR department and want to create a workflow for onboarding a new hire. You could create four boards representing different stages of the onboarding process: Before the first day, On First Day, 30 days in, 60 days in. Each board can have a list of tasks that need to be completed on that board.

Another example can be a Board for writing a book. An author can create the following boards: Planning process and outline, Writing, Design, Editing, Promotional Sales funnel, Publishing. Or, you can use one board per chapter and a different project for each chapter.

The Getting Things Done (GTD) productivity system: Trello is a great companion to the GTD system by allowing you to have separate boards for each of your main lists. Lists can be categorized according to priority or tasks: (Next Actions, @calls, Someday, Big Picture, etc...)

Covey's Time Matrix or The Eisenhower Matrix: How about a Time Matrix board with lists according to Covey's or Eisenhower's Matrix? For the Time Matrix it would look like; Urgent/Important, Urgent/Not Important, Not Urgent/Urgent, Not Urgent/Not important. If you want to model the Eisenhower Matrix, your lists would include; Do First, Schedule, Delegate, Don't Do.

https://trello.com

Pomodoro Apps

The Pomodoro technique is a simple method for helping you keep your focus for a short period of time. Unless you want to use the original Tomato timer, I recommend an app to help you gain discipline and maintain high energy levels. The available apps are simple by default but there a variety of ways to make a 25-minute timer.

I used to struggle a lot with maintaining focus when it came to writing. It was easy to get distracted, and my attention would easily drift off to another topic. When I first heard of this method, I didn't take it seriously. "I mean, 25-minute Focus time followed by a 5-minute break. How could that work?"

When I started my Pomodoro experiment mentioned in the previous chapter, I quickly understood its popularity. The time is short enough to allow you to zero in on one thing and keep your energy levels high.

Here are some suggested apps you can test:

Focus Booster (The Web, Windows, Mac)
https://www.focusboosterapp.com/

Focus Booster provides sliders that allow you to fine-tune the length of your own focus periods and break times. It also offers reports and timesheets so you can measure your productivity and see how long you have worked on each project. The desktop app, included in the free plan, provides a minimized view that floats on top of all your windows but stays out of the way.

Pomodoro Keeper (App)

If a mobile app is what you are looking for, then I recommend Pomodoro Keeper. The timer is simple with a clean interface similar to the traditional egg timer you probably have in your kitchen.

What's great about Pomodoro Keeper is you can easily set and track your Pomodoro goals for the day and see how long until you're rewarded with that longer break. The app has a great "getting started" tutorial that helps you get going quickly. Plus, once you start the timer, it automatically transitions between the break timers and work timers—a feature that was sorely missing from other options.

This is the app that I use. I like the sound of the ticking clock (you have the option to turn it off). At first, I thought it was distracting then I noticed that I began to condition myself to focus when I heard the ticking sound. It was almost like a Freudian experiment. My brain would start to focus on the task at hand once the ticking began.

Marinara Timer (Web)
http://www.marinaratimer.com/

Marinara Timer offers a web-based timer without requiring sign-up. There are three timer options based on your needs; Pomodoro, Custom, and Kitchen.

The Pomodoro mode lets you get started right away with the default 25min/5min timers. If you want to customize the timer lengths, the custom mode lets you tweak things to your liking. The kitchen mode is exactly that, a kitchen timer. You set a time limit, and it counts down to zero.

The distinct thing about Marinara is that it gives you a unique URL for each timer. So if you have an office with a shared screen in the room, you could put the timer up and sync everyone's workflow.

Be Focused Pro (Apple store)

There are apps available for all your Apple devices that synchronize with each other. The app tracks your Pomodoros against your daily target and has some cool notification options. The statistics section of Pomodoro Time Pro shows your progress by day, week, or for a custom time period.

Calendar Apps

Which calendar system are you using for your calendar? Although every mobile system and even email application comes with a calendar option, it may not be the best option for you. There are a variety of options available for you to choose the one that fits best with you.

I highly recommend that you choose a Calendar App that integrates with your Task Management App. This will make prioritizing your day seamless.

Google Calendar

https://www.google.com/calendar

I have to start with one of the most powerful calendars available. Available in both Android and IOS, it is a well thought out time management app. It mimics Google Calendar on your computer and gives you the option to pick from a variety of views.

One of the best options is its ability to sync across all platforms. If you have a Google account, this may be a great option for you.

Readdle's Calendars 5

https://readdle.com/products/calendars5

This is the Calendar app that I use for personal use. I like its simplicity and how it syncs across devices. It has all the great functions of a good calendar app including entering new events in plain speech. It also has a solid task and event management system that syncs easily with the built-in iOS calendar app, as well as Google and iCal.

Cal (Android, iOS: Free)
https://www.any.do/cal/

Cal is the brainchild of the Any.do team, delivering a calendar app that is both functional and gorgeous. Their event creation is done with ease, with Cal attempting to plug in contact invites and location data based on the event name. If you have Any.do as your task management app, then this may be a great option for giving you the ability to sync tasks over from Any.do. The event, day and month views are displayed in front of a selection of themed pictures, which gives the app a compelling visual flair.

Business Calendar 2 (Android)

This has long been an Android fan favorite due to its usability and features. Users can easily switch between a variety of calendar views, from precise daily and weekly calendars, agenda modes for quick summaries, and overarching month calendars. Events are easily marked in colored swatches for easy reference. The app also includes easy task and event creation, and highly configurable widgets give you an easy at-a-glance reference. A Pro upgrade provides extra features such as advanced task management and event templates.

Gmail Chrome Extensions

If you want a quick win, start with your email habits. More on that in the next chapter. Email management can help increase your productivity, or it can be a productivity killer. No mistake about that. If you are able to maximize your time reading, sorting, replying to and filing your emails, you will find yourself with more free time to invest on your Most Important Tasks.

This section focuses only on Gmail Chrome Extensions since it is one of the most widely used email services. There is also a wide variety of options available to choose from. The list provided below is a good place to start.

Note: there are a variety of extensions that allow you to turn your emails into tasks right in your Inbox. I have chosen not to display them here. You can find a great task management app that can be integrated into your Gmail account. However, I don't recommend you use your Inbox for task management.

Boomerang
http://www.boomeranggmail.com/

With Boomerang you can prepare emails and schedule them to be sent at a specified date in the future, as well as get reminders if there was no reply to one of your emails after a specified amount of time. Keeping track of all emails sent and received can be difficult. Boomerang simplifies this ability. It is also extremely popular with Entrepreneurs.

FollowUp CC
https://followup.cc/

To add to the functionality of plugins like Boomerang, FollowUp CC lets you create polite little follow-up emails to be sent to those who haven't given you a reply. You can have these emails sent after a certain amount of time or at a specified date, e.g., after one week if it's not a pressing matter or on the day before a deadline is due.

Unroll.me
https://unroll.me/

This could be a time saver and a headache reliever. If you are like me, you probably have a ton of subscriptions that clog your Inbox. Hopefully, your subscription to LeadGrowDevelop and #5MinMotivation series is not one of them.

I have a number of emails that flood my Inbox daily from the majority of stores and sites that I visited a few times. I used to simply go about deleting my emails without opening them and reading only the ones I wanted to. It simply took too long to click on each email individually to unsubscribe. If this is your process too, think about the amount of time you are spending or wasting.

Now with Unroll. I simply entered my email service, and it quickly told me I had 155 subscriptions. Then it took me less than 10 minutes to go through every one of them and either; Roll up, unsubscribe, or keep in my Inbox. The Roll up option is for those emails you want to read but don't want it cluttering your inbox. You get a daily newsletter style email (you choose morning, afternoon or night) and it gives you one email with all the subscriptions you chose. The important emails that I want to open right away, I kept in my Inbox. In a matter of fewer than 10 minutes, I unsubscribed to 66 emails and Roll-up and Inboxed the rest.

TIME SAVER

CheckerPlus

If you have multiple email accounts, then Check Plus is a great option. It allows you to label and monitor important emails and get notifications with user photos. Too busy to read emails? It can even be set up to read your emails out loud to you. You can run it independent of your browser and get new email alerts even if it is closed.

WiseStamp

https://webapp.wisestamp.com/

WiseStamp gives you that little bit extra in terms of designing your own unique signature, complete with an image, basic information, and links to social media, as well as cool additional features like your last Tweet or Facebook status.

Key Rocket

There are so many keyboard shortcuts that it is impossible for me to remember them all. I pretty much only knew Ctrl-C and V. The advantage to shortcuts is the time it can save you from searching for the function on the top bar.

Key Rocket helps you remember the time-saving shortcuts by notifying you with little pop-ups every time you click on an option that you could have just used a shortcut for. Over time you'll notice that you will start remembering the ones you use most.

Grammarly

https://app.grammarly.com/

I love this extension. It is spell check on steroids. It not only checks your emails and documents for spelling mistakes but verifies grammar, punctuation, sentence style and structure. At the end of the week, you get a summary email on how many words were reviewed as well as your stats on writing accuracy. It can be used as a cool tracker on how many words you write.

ClearBit
https://connect.clearbit.com/

If you're searching for contact information, Clearbit is the Gmail Chrome extension for you. Just plug in Company + Name or Job Title. Clearbit finds their email address (and social profiles), so you can one-click compose an email to them.

The Top Inbox
http://thetopinbox.com/

Another option to Boomerang. You can schedule emails to be sent at a later date or set reminders in your inbox. You can track opens and follow up with email sequences.

Note Taking

About every year, I get frustrated with everything that has cluttered my closets. I then go about packing items, toys or anything else that no longer adds value to my life. I then select items that can be donated or thrown out. After I complete this exercise, I tend to feel so much better and my closets, as well as my children's closets, become organized again, leaving room for only what is necessary.

In David Allen's "Getting Things Done" method of productivity, he mentions the advantages of doing a brain dump. Much like my cleaning exercise, the idea is to get everything out of your brain and onto paper or an online journal in order to declutter your mind. The main difference between a "brain dump" or a spring cleaning is that our brains need this decluttering much more often.

In life, there's a tendency to let the little-undone things build up, and sometimes even big things, too. Usually, these things fall directly under the "important but not urgent" category of stuff you should be doing. They're important things, but without a strict deadline making it easy to postpone.

No matter how big, small, simple or complex an idea is, get it in writing. If you don't write your ideas down, they could leave your head before the end of the day, sometimes even sooner. The advantage in taking notes is that you can later review them, pick the best ideas and turn them into actionable and measurable goals. Getting in the habit of taking notes is a great way to save time from having to remember something later. It also helps in keeping creative ideas fresh. It is not always possible to have a notepad or notebook handy, but you have mobile options as well. There are great online Note applications that can be a great alternative especially with its ability to sync across several devices.

Google Keep
https://keep.google.com/

Google Keep is a syncing notepad that connects to Google Drive. It lets you quickly take and save notes, photos, voice memos, and checklists to Google Drive, and then access them again on any other web-connected device you use. The seamless transition between all Google tools makes this note-taking option hard to resist. Although it may not be as popular as other note taking applications, it is definitely worth a look for its fast service and great voice-recognition.

Evernote
https://evernote.com/

Evernote has long been a leader in this space, although it has been criticized recently for adding excessive features, and most recently, changing its pricing and tiers of service. Regular users no longer have the value proposition of the free service, and power users have a hike in price. Despite these complaints, Evernote remains one of the best note-taking and syncing services. You have several modification options, and it can be used for practically anything, from recording and sharing meetings, to searching for text inside PDFs and keeping a daily diary.

Microsoft OneNote

https://www.onenote.com/

Another option is Microsoft's OneNote. All your notes, including words in pictures, are searchable inside OneNote, and they are stored in the cloud and immediately accessible via the OneNote apps for any platform. If you are an Office user, OneNote may be a better productivity aide than Evernote since it can smartly integrate with the rest of Office.

BEAR

http://www.bear-writer.com/

Bear works on iPhone, iPad, and Mac. You can link notes to each other to build a body of work and use hashtags to organize the way you think. You can import your notes from Evernote if you feel it suits your style better as well as download a Chrome extension. The apps are free to download, but the ability to sync will cost you $15 a year. At the time of this writing, that represents a quarter of what Evernote charges.

Bear uses a simple three-paned design. The largest column is devoted to your current note. A smaller column to the left contains your notes in reverse-chronological order, topped by a search bar. The left-most column contains notes that you've pinned, as well as any tags you've created to organize your notes.

Online File Storage Options

Which Cloud Storage Service is right for you? I don't think it is a question of whether or not you should use an online storage service. It is more a question of choosing the right one. If you are old enough to remember storing files on floppy disks, I think you can agree that we have come a long way. With a Cloud Storage Service, you can view your files from any phone, tablet or computer that's connected to the Internet. The Cloud also provides backup for files, so they never get lost even if your computer crashes. If you have ever lost precious photos from your phone because they weren't backed-up, you probably still feel the pain.

Although USB keys are a great option, the ability to have access to your files no matter which device you are using and without having to carry a USB is a productivity saver.

Here is a guide to the most popular cloud storage services at the time of this writing.

Google Drive
https://www.google.com/drive/

This is the Cloud sharing service that we use where I work. Much more than just a cloud-based storage, Google Drive is a great syncing service as well. It excels at letting you create, edit, store and collaborate on documents. The service is truly impressive in just how far it goes to help you create and edit files, whether you're working solo or as part of a team. Your files can then be worked on from anywhere.

At the time of this writing, Google Drive is free up to 15GB, then goes up in price depending on your storage needs.

Microsoft OneDrive
https://onedrive.live.com/

OneDrive is pre-installed on Windows 10, and it works great on all your devices. Access and share files and photos on PC, Mac, Android, and iOS. If you are using Word or other Microsoft programs, you can easily save all your documents, photos and audio files to OneDrive. However, it has a small storage space compared to other cloud-based storage options, offering a free account up to 5GB

Apple iCloud
http://www.apple.com/icloud/

Apple's cloud-based file-syncing and storage offering iCloud Drive offers a variety of services. Although it is meant for Apple devices, you can also use it in a Web browser too. With the ability to save files to the cloud, iCloud automatically syncs to all devices you sign up for the service.

The service lets you create folders for your files and provides online storage for Apple's productivity apps, Pages, Numbers, and Keynote. Although I use this service to sync my notes and apps on my Apple devices, I still prefer Google's Drive or Microsoft's OneDrive.

DropBox
https://www.dropbox.com/

With the ability to install Dropbox on any computer or mobile device, you can also integrate Dropbox with dozens of other apps. It now supports real-time collaboration for Office Online users, so you and your colleagues can access and edit the same Dropbox file at the same time. Similar to Google Drive, you can see a sharer's changes appear on the screen as they happen.

All the Dropbox apps are free to download, and there are plenty of them, but space is pretty limited if you don't pay. The free personal account starts you out with a meager 2GB.

Box

https://www.box.com/

Although Box is not as known as the other services mentioned, it gives its users a lot of value. Box has taken every possible step to ensure their customers' information is kept safe, including SSL encryption, password protection, and advanced administrative controls for businesses. Employers are able to set up role-based permissions for their employees or adjust permissions by individual user.

You can keep all your communication centralized in Box by posting any comments you have directly on the file. Mentioning a team member by name sends them an email notification so they can instantly see your own comment and respond. The Box interface also contains an activity feed, so you're always aware of what edits and updates others have made to the files stored in the cloud. In addition to all this, Box integrates with Google Docs so multiple people can edit documents in real time.

Box offers free accounts, paid personal accounts, and business-grade accounts. At 10GB, a free Box personal account comes with five times as much as space as a free Dropbox account's 2GB.

Time Saving Apps that Will Increase Your Productivity

In this section, I review some great options available to simplify a variety of tasks. Improving your productivity can be applied to several areas of your life and not just to task management. While you cannot buy time, you can certainly get tools to manage it better and use it most productively.

Technology has bombarded us with countless tools for managing our work and home life as well as providing options to increase productivity levels. Let's take a look at which of the tools will set your productivity levels soaring high by helping you better manage your time and schedule.

Text Expanders

Despite all the available multimedia formats, plain old text still takes up most of our time. Just think about all the time you spend on emails and reports. Most of your time in the office is still probably spent on typing large volumes of text. This is where text expanders come in handy. They allow you to assign shortcuts and macros to text actions, saving you time on typing emails, documents, and texting.

Imagine all the time you can save in avoiding repetitive tasks. Just think about how many times you have typed out your home address over the past year? It's a string of around 30 characters that takes perhaps eight seconds to write. What if you could type your address with just three characters: @ad. That's what makes text expansion apps so magical: they transform abbreviations into custom lines of text instantly. Or what if you can create a shortcut for email responses? You can even create custom email responses with a simple code.

Think of them as cheat codes for your most-typed phrases.

Some available options:

PhraseExpander
https://www.phraseexpander.com/

Use PhraseExpander to trigger actions by typing abbreviations. This can be through inserting a piece of text, displaying a fill-in template, launching an application or a website. Once you have defined a set of abbreviations, PhraseExpander monitors what you are typing and quietly suggests words, phrases, and actions as you type. You can use templates to generate and customize sentences in a few clicks.

This is a very good program, fit for professional use. There is a 21-day free trial, $50 for Standard edition, $149 for Professional edition.

Phrase Express
http://www.phraseexpress.com/

PhraseExpress has three main functions: Word Corrections, Clipboard Cache, and Local File. Each of these can be configured and hotkeyed independently. Word Corrections requires a dictionary to be downloaded separately for free, available in English, French, German, Dutch, Italian and Portuguese. By default, Clipboard Cache is activated by pressing CTRL+ALT+V and remembers up to 20 separate text entries you copied, but this can be easily changed to virtually unlimited. Local File is the main function of the program and replaces the text noted in the "Autotext" box with whatever is in the "Phrase content" box.

TextExpander

https://textexpander.com/

TextExpander apps cost nothing but work only when there's an active monthly or yearly subscription. Further, the company's website becomes a required hub for all users, whether they sync and share or not. This is a popular option amongst Entrepreneurs.

Pricing starts at $4.16 billed monthly.

Online Automation Tools

Sometimes it is easy to forget how far we have come in such a short time. Depending on how old you are, you may even remember the slow, mind-numbing internet connection of dial-up or when your only option in watching a TV series was on an actual TV.

There are several advantages that advancing technologies brought us. Besides access to more information than has ever been possible, we can use these advantages to increase our productivity.

Online Automation tools are not only valuable for Business owners or Entrepreneurs but for personal productivity as well. Your greatest constraint is often your time, and the following automation tools can help reduce several time constraints.

IFTTT

https://ifttt.com/

IFTTT is both a website and a mobile app that launched in 2010 and has the slogan "Put the Internet to work for you." The idea is that you use IFTTT to automate everything from your favorite apps and websites to app-enabled accessories and smart devices.

You create chains of simple conditional statements, called applets. An applet is triggered by changes that occur within another web service. IFTTT currently supports more than 110 services (also called "channels") including Android devices and Apple iOS apps like Reminders and Photos, as well as websites like Facebook, Instagram, Flickr, Tumblr, Google Calendar, Google Drive, Etsy, Feedly, Foursquare, LinkedIn, SoundCloud, WordPress, YouTube, and more.

Some examples of applets you can create with IFTTT:

- Send an email message if the IFTTT user tweets using a certain hashtag.
- Track your work hours in Google Calendar.
- Automatically turn your Android device's WiFi on when you get home
- Save photos you're tagged in on Facebook to a Dropbox folder
- Sync all your new iOS Contacts to a Google Spreadsheet
- Mute your Android phone when you arrive at work

At the time of this writing, IFTTT is a free to use service, but they are working on Premium options.

Zapier

https://zapier.com/

Zapier is another web automation app. With Zapier you can build Zaps which can automate parts of your business or life. A Zap is a blueprint for a task you want to do over and over. In other words, a Zap looks like this: "When I get a new thing in A, do this other thing in B." The first part is the Trigger and the second part is the Action.

Zapier supports hundreds of apps. You can mix and match triggers and actions to automate just about anything. There is a free plan available allowing for five integrations and syncing is only done every 5 hours. If you need instant notifications, IFTTT is a better choice (if your desired services are offered). Or pay for a work plan starting at $20/month at the time of this writing.

One of the very popular features of IFTTT, shared "recipes" is not available in Zapier but all in all, this could be a great tool to add to your arsenal of automating apps.

Password Manager Apps

With ongoing security threats, the days of using the same passwords all the time are over. Forget 1234 or any other easy password reminder, and please don't save a document on your desktop with your passwords.

After a full day conference, I attended, we carpooled with our out of town attendees and went out for supper. We all left our laptops in the trunks of our cars and entered the restaurant to eat. *"I know, not very smart. I think you know where this is headed."* When we left the restaurant, my colleague had her car broken into, and three laptops from her trunk were taken. An out of country guest had saved all her passwords including banking on her desktop. It didn't take long before a withdrawal was made from her account.

Nowadays with everything needing a password, it can be a nightmare to have to remember them all. Grab one of these apps to manage your passwords across your devices and secure your digital life.

LastPass (Mac, Window, iOS, Android)

https://www.lastpass.com/

The Free LastPass has a bold new online interface, and its new features include a Sharing Centre to manage shared passwords and Emergency Access to hand down your passwords to your heirs. These new features put the free LastPass ahead of even many of its for-pay competitors.

LastPass Premium competes as one of the best online password managers. It has every critical feature and supports all popular operating systems, browsers and mobile devices.

1Password (Mac, Windows, iOS, Android)

https://1password.com/

1Password started off as a Mac-only product but has expanded to cover iOS, Android, and Windows. You can try it for free but has monthly plans for individuals ($2.99) and family ($4.99).

1Password allows you to easily generate strong passwords for every site you visit and is secure as long as you can think of a strong master password. At least you will now only have one password to remember.

News Aggregator Apps

How much surfing, researching, or reading do you do online? When you are pressed for time, you don't always have time to read all the articles you found of interest. If an interesting article has caught your eye and you don't want to lose it, you can use a News Aggregator App to store all your favorite posts.

Feedly

https://feedly.com/

As a user of Feedly, I can attest to its ease of use. Instead of giving you a massive list for you to scroll through, Feedly breaks your content feed up into manageable chunks. It provides you with suggestions based on your subjects of interest and organizes topics into subheadings. Feedly will show you the latest stories from each folder.

Pocket
https://getpocket.com/

As their saying goes, "when you find something you want to view later, put it in "Pocket." Put articles, videos or pretty much anything into Pocket. You can save directly from your browser or from apps like Twitter and Flipboard. You can Pocket from your Web Browser, email or from a variety of over 1500+ Apps.

Ready to view? Then just look in Pocket. It syncs to your iPhone, iPad, Android, Kobo, or Web Browser. You don't even need an Internet connection.

Flipboard
https://flipboard.com/

Flipboard makes the entire reading process as stylish as possible and integrates all your social media accounts like Twitter and Instagram. Its most recent update now features video, giving your content more variety.

Mileage Trackers

When I first started tracking my mileage for business purposes, I would often forget to log my starting mileage and then my ending mileage. It was a habit that took a while to get going. I often had to rely on my memory to remember where I was throughout the week then use Google maps to calculate my mileage. Talk about needing to brain dump. The energy required to remember to track mileage on a consistent basis is not necessary. There is no need to clog your mind with unnecessary data.

When it comes to tracking mileage, there are great options available to make this process automatic, reduce human error and increase productivity. Here are three great options currently available.

Mileage Tracker Plus (iOS)

Mileage tracker plus is designed to help you quickly and easily keep track of expenses incurred as you use your vehicle. Use this application to keep accurate logs and generate summary reports.

Mile IQ (iOS, Android)

https://www.mileiq.com/

A swipe is all it takes to mark trips as business, personal, medical, charity or any customer category you wish. Log any additional details needed for reporting mileage expenses to your employer or deducting mileage on your tax return. You can also bulk and automate classification options.

Mile IQ is the most expensive option in this little roundup, but it's also one of the most polished and easy-to-use apps.

TripLog

https://triplogmileage.com/

Their website shows you options based on your needs. You can start with a 30-day trial run for new users, allowing you to test the app for free. Then you can choose one of their main plans; self-employed, or enterprise.

The automated mileage tracking is more comprehensive here than in either of the other apps, at least in terms of how it engages. You can choose when it engages such as when it is plugged into the car or when a Bluetooth connection is made. You can even have it engaged within a specific time period or when it detects movement above a certain mileage.

Contact List Apps

Think about all the different contacts you have across all your platforms. How do you keep them all organized? Bottom line is that the contact app that comes with your phone may not meet all your needs. If networking is an important part of your every day, then it is essential to find a tool to manage all your contacts. Nowadays, we don't just have a phone number or email address tied to our names. There are all those social media accounts that could make a difference in connecting with the right people.

Contact Cleanup and Merge (iOS: Free)
If you are only looking to clean up your contact list, then your first step should be to find a good contact cleaner and merge application. When I downloaded this app on my iPhone, I had 21 duplicate contacts. I don't even know how that happened. Contact Cleanup and Merge for iOS provides one-click removal of duplicate contacts. You can also restore deleted contacts if a mistake is made. It has smart filters including merging contacts with duplicate phone numbers, email, and names as well as contacts without phone numbers or email.

Sync.ME (Android, iOS: Free)
https://sync.me/

Sync.ME makes managing your contacts simple. This app pulls contact information from your Google+, Facebook, LinkedIn or Twitter accounts to keep your contacts automatically updated with the latest profile photos and other related contact details. It can also identify unknown phone calls and warns you of annoying SPAM calls.

Premium features allow you to merge duplicate contacts, create backup files for your contacts and background sync.

Cloze (Android, iOS: Free)
https://www.cloze.com/

Cloze refers to its app as a relationship management app. It pulls from your apps to automatically create one view of every person and company. The app not only gives you contact details but a complete history of every interaction (email, phone calls, meetings, notes, files, social and messages). For team projects, it gives you one team-wide view of all communication for every deal and projects.

FullContact (iOS, Android, Gmail: Free)
https://www.fullcontact.com/

FullContact wants to be the one that replaces your address book. It brings together your phone and social media contacts, merging contacts and information. Users can add customized tags to easily create groups and search through the address book. From there, you can quickly call, email or view the social media profiles. Contacts can be backed up in the cloud, and automatically sync across FullContact for iOS, Web, and Gmail.

CHAPTER THIRTEEN – Email Strategies That Help Bring Your Inbox to Zero

*"**Put** my phone on no notifications. Therefore, I am no longer purposefully ignoring people. I'm currently premeditating it."*

Ring, Ding, or "you've got mail." Whatever your email notification is, it can be extremely distracting. Then you look up and see that you have another incoming email message. You ask yourself, "what's another email message added to my current list of 200 emails?" If you find yourself in this situation often, it is time to change your strategy.

How does email affect your productivity? Before you can answer that question, you need to ask yourself how much time you spend reading, composing and responding to email?

I used to feel overwhelmed with the amount of email and responses that I used to receive. Mostly because of those emails and in turn requests, were not in my original plan. I found myself rearranging my priorities to respond to the priorities of others. I knew, that if I were to stay on my course, I needed to do things differently.

How do you create an effective work routine? Choosing what you want it to be rather than let others dictate it.

Here are some email statistics, according to the Radicati Group.
- In 2016, email remains the most common form of communication in the business space.
- Email use is growing in the business sector, and by 2018, business email will account for over 139.4 billion emails sent and received per day.
- Business users sent and received on average 121 emails a day in 2014, and this is expected to grow to 140 emails a day by 2018.

These statistics do not include personal and spam emails that one might receive throughout the day. Let's be conservative and say that about 20% of your business emails require a response. That means that an extra 28 tasks just got added to your to-do list.

Can you feel your overwhelm meter start to rise?

If you don't have a system in place to control your email, it can be a huge deterrent to your productivity.
The good news is that there are strategies that you can put in place to help you regain control of your Inbox.

5 Email Strategies to Help Bring Your Inbox To Zero:

1. Consolidate your Emails

How many email addresses do you have? The more email addresses you have, the more follow-up you need to do. Try to consolidate your email addresses as much as you can. Do you belong to any Forums or communities? Set it up so that any direct messages get sent to one of your email addresses. This allows follow up to be easier, without having to log into multiple sites. My Twitter direct messages get forwarded to one of my email accounts which make it easier to manage.

I have three accounts; business, personal and one for this blog. Any more would affect my productivity.

2. Create a Schedule for Processing Emails

The first thing I used to do in the morning was read my emails. The problem with this was that I had my schedule already planned. Reading my emails often took me away from something else that I had planned to do. Often, those other things were on my priority list.

A best practice is to review your agenda for the day first and then work on your Most Important Tasks for the day. Emails should come only after your most important tasks are set in motion. Create a schedule for processing emails (i.e., 9h 12h 16h) and set a time limit. I now set a 30 min. time limit per session.

3. The 5 Minute Rule

How do you process your emails? Do you read through all of them once, then go back to those that require action? This means that you are reading the same email more than once reducing the time it takes to process all your messages.

Try practicing the 5-minute rule: When you read an email, and the action required takes less than 5 minutes to complete, Do It. This avoids you having to go back to it later and maybe forgetting about it. The more you can read your emails just once, the better your productivity.

4. The 3D's and F

Follow these next steps, and with practice, you will quickly go through your emails.

With each email, ask yourself this question, "Is it Actionable"?

Does it require an action from you?

If Actionable, follow these steps:

Do It- If it will take you less than 5 minutes

Delegate It – Can you defer this email to someone else who can successfully complete it?

If it is not Actionable, follow these steps:

File It – If the message is informational in nature and that you will require later, file it. Word of caution, don't create too many files. Try to keep it to less than five folders for quicker reference after.

Delete it – If it is not information that you will need later and if it is not actionable, delete it. I know several people that have an issue with deleting email feeling like they might "one day" require the information. Learn to keep your Inbox lean. Learn to Delete.

5. 3 Things to Keep In Mind When Sending Emails

This last strategy is more about other people's inbox more than your own. If you start putting these things into practice, maybe you can set an example for your office.

Here are three things that you need to think about before you send an email:

(i) Keep it Short. Become a fan of bullet points. Learn to get your point across without the novel.

(ii) Don't overestimate the importance of the Subject Line. Did you ever get an email with no subject line? Subject lines are great ways to reference an email you want to get back to later. A practical way to send the receiver an idea of what you need from them is to add the following information at the beginning of the email.

FYI – information only

Action Required – Stating your need for an action.

Urgent – Self-explanatory

To do by – When you need an action before a certain date. Should only be sent to those reporting to you.

(iii) Think twice before you forward, cc, bcc or reply all. Are you a reply all kind of person? Maybe you shouldn't be. Ask yourself if this person really needs to receive a cc or bcc.

Respect other people's time so that they, in turn, can respect yours. Think about the emails you are sent a copy of. What percentage of those emails do you really need to be informed of? Determine if you should copy someone else in an email by asking the following question, "Does the person I want to copy need this information to directly perform his duties? "Will this information positively impact the recipient's performance?" If the answer to both questions is no, avoid the "double arrow/reply all."

PART IV: THE PLAN

CHAPTER FOURTEEN – Out of Overwhelm Came the Productivity Equation

"Success has a simple formula:
do your best, and people may like it. "
Sam Ewing

I was having supper with some friends who I hadn't seen in a while. I had my son with me who was four years old at the time. Either through excitement, but most probably due to boredom, he knocked over his juice. I automatically reached over for the cup but was too late. The juice spilled on the table and was cascading quickly onto the floor. Not wanting to cause a mess, I tried to catch the juice with my cupped hands. Unsuccessfully, the juice rushed through my fingers and created the mess I was trying to avoid. I managed to save about 10% of the liquid.

When it came to productivity, my life felt similar. I found myself always scrambling at the end of the day or week to accomplish more tasks without really stopping to think if they were the right tasks. Much like the juice overflowing onto the floor, no matter how much I tried to maintain control of everything, I found myself losing in areas that were most important. Needless to say, Overwhelm was a feeling I knew well. After multiple trials and failures, I couldn't figure out a method that worked for me on a consistent basis. When I finally figured out the Productivity equation, things started falling into place.

This chapter summarizes my productivity equation. My winning system for getting the right things done with the greatest return on investment, without sacrificing what is important. Ironically, as I mentioned at the beginning of this book, when I started this book writing journey, my responsibilities started to increase more than ever before. The extra workload of writing a book was added to my increased responsibilities of going from 13 stores to at one point 43 plus being part of 3 committees.

The saying, "if you want something to be done, give it to a busy person," should be replaced with,

"If you want something to be done right, give it to a productive person."

My career was taking off which eventually led me to getting a Regional Sales Director position all while continuing to work on this book. Funny how life works. Once I became consistent with my habits, I found myself managing more projects and tasks than ever before. Without the Overwhelm.

Why am I using the end of the book to describe what works best for me? Why didn't I start with this in the beginning and give you the shortcut? Throughout this book, I hoped to have taken you through a journey of options. To shed some light on the best habits and systems that would contribute the most to your productivity.

This is your journey, and hopefully, this books helped identify your vision for creating your own productivity equation. Once this book is complete, I will begin to work on a course that helps you build your own productivity equation step by step. Depending on when you read this book, it might already be created.

You can always find out about my latest projects on my blog www.LeadGrowDevelop.com.

This chapter is about how I created my Productivity Plan. Take it as a guide to help you create yours. Where to start may feel overwhelming on its own which is why I tried to break it down into steps of an equation, taken one at a time.

My Plan

The first step in the equation and the most important....

Your Mindset

No productivity system in the world, no matter how great, works on its own. There is no magical productivity system. You need to master your mindset first, then....

Create New Habits

Once you are able to Shift your Mindset, then the next step should be determining which habits you need to create that will contribute to your productivity. Trying to change too many things at once is not the best strategy. Work on one habit at a time. I cannot overemphasize this enough. Building habits is hard enough without trying to build too many of them at once. Start small. If you want to exercise 1 hour a day, start with building a habit of 10 minutes a day. Get in as many wins as possible and once you create the momentum, then look to other habits. Once your habits are formed, you can create your structure that compliments your habits and enhances your productivity. Once you find one that works for you, it can be used as your framework. Although it is a framework, your system is a tool and not a law. It can be modified and adjusted according to your needs.

My Productivity Equation: Mindset + Habits + Systems

So what works for me? The following pages summarize my productivity equation. This is what allowed me to stay consistently productive despite an increasing workload and responsibility load.

My Mindset:

My first step was in determining my personal philosophy and what mattered most to me. I imagined myself 20 years in the future having a conversation with my two sons about the previous 20 years. I jotted down on a piece of paper what I believed that conversation would look like. I wrote down as much information as possible: where I was, what achievements I was proud of, how I felt etc… This helped me determine what would be important in the future. Not surface importance but real importance. Sometimes what seems to be of importance today does not seem so important in the future.

I then jotted down the areas of my life that I believe would remain important. The achievements I hoped to achieve. I broke down my goals into categories and then chose 1-2 big goals per category.

I had written down goals for key areas in my life: family, personal development, career, Blog and Spiritual. I did a complete brain dump and jotted down as many goals I could think of. This was a fun exercise as I let my imagination run wild. At the end of my exercise, I went through all the goals once more and circled the main goals that I wanted to focus on in the short term. I kept it to 1-2 big goals and focused first on two key areas. I didn't want to set too many goals at once until I got the process right.

"You can do everything you want, just not all at once."

Now that my big goals were clear, I needed to determine how I would achieve them. Productivity is about being successful at completing tasks in a timely manner that brings you closer to your Most Important Goals. In order to do so, I needed to build the habits that would get me there.

My Habits:

When it came to creating the right habits that would launch my Productivity journey and create a key step in the Productivity Equation, there are four that made the biggest difference. I didn't attempt to build all four major habits at once. Well, that's not true. At the beginning of my journey, I was ambitious and thought I could build a whole bunch of habits at the same time. Guess what happened? They didn't stick.

I realized that I need to start smaller. I wanted to pick a habit, get a win and then build from there.

Habit 1: Eliminate Time Vampires

I started with identifying and then working on eliminating my Time Vampires. I had a lot. I first needed to identify what was zapping my energy the most. I narrowed it down to two major themes, the people I was surrounding myself with and the way I managed distractions.

Your environment and the people you choose to surround yourself with can be a major energy zapper if you are not careful. It was a philosophy that I had heard several times before but hadn't taken the time to actually do a "people audit." The idea of auditing the people in your life may seem cruel. Bottom line, if there are people in your life that are a negative drain and you take no action, you are being cruel to yourself.

When I took the time to analyze where and with whom I spent my time, I began to see a pattern between my productivity and energy levels. I realized that when I spent time with certain people who spent most of their time complaining, I would feel tired after and be less productive. Their stories would even stay in my mind for a while.

Sometimes, you just need to make some decisions. I am not saying to give up on your family or those closest to you, although sometimes it may be the only answer. What is important is to set boundaries with these people and decide what type of relationship you want to have.

First, you need to identify who is sucking your energy. Take some time to grab a piece of paper and a pen. Write down the names of the people you spend the most time with.

How to Identify a Vampire

Ask yourself these questions, "when I'm with this person, do I..."

☐

- Feel more confident and energetic?
- Feel calm and relaxed?
- Look forward to seeing them again?
- Get excited when I see their name on my phone or inbox?
- In the past, when I've shared my ambitions with this person, did I come out of the conversation feeling motivated to get going on with my project? Or, did I feel discouraged and start doubting my ideas?
- Has this person helped me in any way to develop a skill or personality trait?

Once you've identified potential negative influencers or "time vampires," you have one of three choices. Decide whether or not you need to do the following with this person.

Increase Association - If this person contributes to your positive energy and personal development, find ways in which you can spend more time with him or her.

Limited Association – Sometimes cutting this person completely from your life is not an option. In this situation, try to limit your association. When dealing with a family member, this may not always be an easy situation but may be necessary. You don't have to eliminate them completely from your life but keep the visits to Birthdays and Holidays.

No Association - These are the people that are not just draining but sucking your energy. They make you doubt your abilities or discourage you from trying to go after your goals.

Once I made the choice to work on eliminating my time vampires, I had a big choice to make. Do nothing or be serious about becoming more productive. I knew that I had to set boundaries with the people I had placed in my limited association pile. I had to learn to say "no" to their priorities, so I can say "yes" to mine. This is not about being rude, it's about doing what's right for you and the person. Funny thing about "time vampires" is that they get their energy from sucking it out of others. Most of the time, they don't even realize it. By being intentional about the people you surround yourself with, you might even help the "negative" people in your life realize the consequences of their behaviors.

This habit took a while to build but created a lot of positive change. In a way, it even enhanced my relationship with my network because I was being more transparent and intentional about my choices. Some people even "thanked" me for being honest with how I felt and didn't even realize the impact they were having on others.

My next biggest "Time Vampire" was the distractions I allowed to take over my life. This required me to put the right systems in place to help me build this habit. I will cover more of that in the Systems part of the book.

The biggest distractions I focused on managing or eliminating?
- Scheduling time to read and answer my emails. Hint, it is never the first task I do in a day.
- Putting my phone on silence when I am having a conversation with one of my direct reports. This helped increase my productivity during One-on-One's and store visits as well as their level of engagement.
- Being intentional to eliminate distraction when it is Family time.

This meant no cell phone or tablet when we are together.

- Another big win for me was choosing where and when I spent my time in Social Media. Instead of dividing my free time amongst the seven sites I had an account in, I invested my time on the sites where my audience was spending their time.

Habit 2: MIT for the Day – Win the Day before it even starts

This one took me a while to build before I mastered Habit 1. Once I learned to eliminate distractions, it was easier to focus on my Most Important Tasks for the day. This habit was an immense contributor to my productivity. It relied on two things; building a strong morning routine and creating an end of day routine.

Creating a Morning Routine is not a new concept and was made famous by Hal Elrod and his, "Miracle Morning" book. I read his book and adapted my morning routine to what works best for me. I am a strong believer that if you start your morning right, you can get more done before noon than most people get done throughout the day.

There is an important step that cannot be missed before you even get out of bed. What you want to accomplish in the morning and the first half of your day must be so clear that you accomplish your tasks almost automatically. To succeed at this, you must first create a process that is easy to implement and becomes ingrained into your productivity system.

We will go more into my morning routine and MIT during the Right Systems part of this chapter.

It is important to note that the more I practice my productivity equation, the more productivity habits I can add. I don't attempt to add another habit unless I have mastered all my previous habits first.

Here's what my Productivity Equation looks like so far:

Right Mindset (zeroed in on personal philosophy and areas of priority)
+
Right Habits (Eliminate Time Vampires + determine MIT for the day)

Now for the third part of the equation, the Systems.

My Systems:

My productivity system is separated into how I manage projects and how I manage my day to day priorities.

Starting right.
One of my most effective systems is built upon my MIT habit already mentioned. It starts with winning the day before it even begins. Every day before I can consider my day as over, I spend some time reviewing what I accomplished during the day. I then think and plan my morning and first half of my day for the following day. I determine what will be my Most Important Tasks for the following day and plan on how I will accomplish it. I then write out my morning routine including my first 2-3 tasks for the day.

Here is how it may look like planning my morning routine and setting my MIT for the following day:
At the end of each day and before I shut down for the day, I **plan my Most Important Tasks to start with**. I write down what my key priorities are for the next day and add it to my task management system.
I use the **Todoist task management** system and keep tasks to only what I can accomplish for the day. I then note what my MIT tasks are

and ensure I start my work day with those. Sometimes scheduling priorities such as meetings make it difficult to start with my MIT tasks. If it is not possible to start with them, then I put it in my calendar for the first free space I have.

Once I determine my MIT tasks, I jot down the order in which I want to accomplish my remaining tasks for the day. I tend to be most aggressive before noon and more flexible in the afternoon where I reserve free time for unscheduled tasks (phone calls, follow-ups, etc....). My MIT tasks can also be seen as my Quadrant 2 tasks from Covey's Time Matrix.

My morning routine for a typical work week:
- 5:30 a.m. Wake up
- 10-minute workout or wake up routine
- Shower, eat while listening to a Podcast
- Get Kids going for the day
- Get dressed
- Start on my MIT for the day

While there are plenty of articles available teaching the benefits of accomplishing 14 things before 8 am, I chose a different path. It may work for a large percentage of the population, but I found that it also did the reverse to another percentage of the population. If you are so stressed out because you want to ensure your morning is as productive as possible and cram as much into your first 2 hours as possible, then you might be missing the point.

Take a look at your morning routine. Does it get you ramped up, or stressed out? If it is already working for you, then don't worry about changing anything. My only recommendation is adding your MIT tasks to the start of your workday. If your morning routine is not working? What about it doesn't work?

If you find yourself rushing in the morning to get ready, try waking up 20 minutes earlier. Or, preparing some of your morning tasks the night before (kid's lunches are a great example). If you normally wake up at 7 am, you don't need to be part of the 5 am crowd the next day. Try 15 minutes earlier to start. A lot can get done in 15 minutes if you plan it right.

The next step is to figure out what gets you going in the morning? A cold shower? A quick workout or listening to your favorite songs? Make that part of your routine to get your energy levels high.

"Use what works for others to inspire ideas, but you don't need to copy them. What works for others won't necessarily work for you."

Focus time:

When I am working on my MIT tasks, I use the **Pomodoro technique** to help me stay focused and eliminate distractions. This particularly works well for my writing as well as reducing procrastination. Sometimes, when I just don't feel motivated to start, committing to a small Pomodoro usually gets my momentum going and makes it easier to keep going.

I love the **"Don't Break the Chain"** technique for building habits. It was particularly useful for my keeping up with my blog. I was constantly struggling to get ahead and build a bank of blog posts as back-up. Once, I started this technique; I found myself motivated to see how many days I can go without breaking the chain. At first, I would get 3-4 days of consistent writing going but then started finding myself with 10-12 day chains. Since I have a full-time job as Sales Director, before starting this technique, I would find myself tired at the end of a long day and put off writing until the weekend. Now, I commit to at least one

Pomodoro cycle of 33 min. in order for me to mark that X on the calendar.

Calendars. I try to schedule everything even if it is not an appointment. I schedule my MIT on my calendar app and commit to the time as if it was a Doctor's appointment.

Projects:

Projects are managed similarly to the SCRUM methodology using a Kanban board. I have been using Trello to ensure that I come in line with my project deadlines. For example, I created a board to help me organize and complete this book. It really helped me to organize and prioritize all the steps required for idea creation to writing, editing, marketing, and publishing. If you want further information on the Scrum method, you can read my blog post on the topic reviewing the methodology as well as the main book on the topic, "Scrum: The Art of Doing Twice the Work in Half the Time," by Jeff Sutherland.

You can read it on

http://www.leadgrowdevelop.com/11-step-process-of-agile-scrum-methodology/

Does it sound too simple? The simplest steps added up can take you far. The success of the Productivity Equation is the combined effect of the four steps.

Productivity Equation = Right Mindset + Right Habits + Right System + Your Plan

PRODUCTIVITY EQUATION

Adding all four steps increases your chances of success in maintaining and achieving Productivity. Find out what your Productivity Equation is and make it work for you.

Now, the only thing left is for you to **Create Your Own Plan.**

References

Covey, Stephen. n.d. *Amazon 7 Habits.*
   https://www.amazon.com/Habits-Highly-Effective-People-Powerful/dp/1451639619/ref=sr_1_1?s=books&ie=UTF8&qid=1456245561&sr=1-1&keywords=seven+habits+of+highly+effective+people.

Dictionary, Business. n.d. *Business Dictionary.*

—. n.d. *Business Dictionary.*
   http://www.businessdictionary.com/definition/productivity.html.

n.d. *Merriam Webster.* https://www.merriam-webster.com/dictionary/mind%E2%80%93set.

Torres, Elita. n.d. *Blueprint for Success.*
   http://www.leadgrowdevelop.com/personal-development-topics-your-personal-blueprint-for-success/.

About the Author

Elita Torres has over 25 years of experience in leading and developing teams in a variety of fields including Electronics, Appliances, and Fashion.

She started her blog on **www.LeadGrowDevelop.com** with the intention to inspire others to go after their dreams and provide tools and resources to help them along the way.

Although her role as a leader is an important one, her most important role remains her role as a parent and wife.

Mother of two boys and married for 19 years, her greatest legacy she hopes to leave behind is one for her family. "To believe that it is possible, learn from what is lost and add value where you can."

www.LeadGrowDevelop.com

Thanks for reading! If you enjoyed this book, reviews are the best way to let me know. Please add a short review on Amazon and let me know what you thought!

Free Resources

Get the Productivity Lessons Resource as a Thank You for Purchasing my book:

A collection of 5 key articles to start you on your Productivity Journey.

Click the link

https://leadgrowdevelop.lpages.co/productivity-equation-resources

PRODUCTIVITY EQUATION

www.ingramcontent.com/pod-product-compliance
Lightning Source LLC
Chambersburg PA
CBHW071029240526
45469CB00006BD/2140